Teachers and the Law

Teachers and the Law

Kim Insley

Institute of Education
University of London

First published in 2008 by the Institute of Education, University of London
20 Bedford Way, London WC1H 0AL

www.ioe.ac.uk/publications

British Library Cataloguing in Publication Data
A catalogue record for this publication is available from the British Library

ISBN 978 0 85473 774 1

Kim Insley asserts the moral right to be identified as the author of this work.

Page make up by Keystroke, 28 High Street, Tettenhall, Wolverhampton
Printed by DSI Colourworks

Contents

Foreword

It's really important for all teachers to understand their legal position, especially in these litigious times. There's a lot of folklore around about how the law relates to school life. As a new teacher you need to know the legal framework within which you work not only because it is a standard that you have to meet for qualified teacher status but because it will inform all that you do.

This book won't give you easy answers but something much better: it will get you thinking! It will help you understand the principles upon which the legal framework stands in five key areas: the statutory basis for education; curriculum and assessment; equal opportunities; health and safety; and employment. This will help you clarify what is law, what is guidance and what is good practice – and the difference between these. You'll also know where to get up-to-date information.

The language that laws are framed in can be hard to understand. For instance, section 93 of the Education and Inspections Act 2006 says that staff can use 'such force as is reasonable in the circumstances' to prevent pupils from committing an offence, causing injury to themselves or others, or inhibiting good order and discipline. But what is 'reasonable force'? The case studies in this book will help you think through issues like this and base your decisions on common sense, teaching expertise and legal knowledge.

Of course the law doesn't just cover your relationship with pupils. Many schools try to fob new teachers off with a temporary or fixed-term rather than a permanent contract. But regardless of whether you work on a full-time, part-time, temporary or permanent basis, once you've completed 12 months of continuous service with the same employer, you have the right not to be unfairly dismissed.

So, you see that the law is not a dry boring subject but one which is essential for all teachers – and this book gives you a good grounding.

Sara Bubb
November 2007

Acknowledgements

Many people have been instrumental in seeing this book achieve publication, but really there are only four acknowledgements.

The first has to be the Open Learning Part-time Primary PGCE Course Team, past and present, at the Institute of Education. The original material was written with Jane Spencer, Course Leader (1998–2003) and Sue Collins, Professional Issues tutor (2000–2001) and developed from the Primary PGCE materials.

Secondly, the student teachers who have accessed the material and given feedback.

On a major update of the material following the new standards for Initial Teacher Education (February 2002) I asked my lawyer husband, Ian, to help me understand how new legislation should be seen in the light of previous legislation. As a construction lawyer he had little knowledge of education law, but was able to help, and he suggested I write a book. He has helped me realise this. He has proved to be a critical reader, adding his own knowledge and understanding to the book. And we are still married!

Finally, I must thank my friends (and colleagues) Chris Saleh (Deputy Course Leader, Open Learning Part-time Primary PGCE), Sylvia Lucas (Nurture Group tutor, Institute of Education), Astrid Hennessy and Lesley Staggs for all their support.

Introduction

There has always been a legal framework for the provision of public services and in recent years education has now acquired one of the most comprehensive and complete of them all. The education system has recently entered a new era of regulation. Following the 1944 Education Act no major Act of Parliament relating to schools was passed until 1980, but this was then followed by ten Acts culminating in the Education and Inspections Act 2006 as well as numerous other Acts which also apply to education, such as the Data Protection Act and the Violent Crime Acts. It is likely that this trend will continue and teachers will need to be aware of how the changing law is affecting them.

With today's electronic communication it is much easier to access information. Search engines such as Google enable this access, and within the teaching profession online support websites such as TeacherNet, the Department for Children, Schools and Families (DCSF) and the Qualifications and Curriculum Authority (QCA) offer their own search tools. This electronic communication has no limits, it seems, and often teachers can spend long hours searching for information and finding too much. A search may not offer the answers sought for and can result in frustration with the disappointing results.

This book is not designed to answer all your questions about the law and how it applies to education. It would certainly be out of date as soon as it was published if it tried to. Its aim is to identify a pathway through the plethora of information and statutory requirements in order to enable you to reflect on practice. To facilitate this each chapter includes examples of incidents, all based on real situations. You may find it useful to consider your own possible response to these situations before reading the discussion of what an appropriate response might be and how this could be viewed in law.

Another aim of this book is to explore the law and how it might apply to teachers in key areas of their work. It will consider how professionals should approach the law, reflecting on how legislation should be considered, and so be useful long after its publication.

HOW LEGISLATION WORKS

The law is dynamic in that it can always change and evolve. The 'law' is found in Acts of Parliament and the decisions of judges. This applies in the three different legal 'units' of England and Wales, Northern Ireland and Scotland. However, the law may be different in Scotland particularly as the legal system there is founded on a different basis. The introduction of regional assemblies has also resulted in differences in the law in Wales and Scotland.

Acts of Parliament may set the law themselves (e.g. the Theft Acts set out the criminal offence of theft) or they may give power to government ministers to make the law by Statutory Instruments. Even these may not provide the rules that teachers need to know about on a day-to-day basis, such as what should be in the curriculum or when a pupil may be excluded.

A Statutory Instrument may empower Local Authorities (LAs) or school governors to make the detailed rules.

Decisions of judges are also a source of law. Judges cannot change Acts of Parliament but they can interpret the words to decide what Parliament meant or to decide issues which are not covered properly (or at all) by an Act of Parliament. Decisions of judges on points of law are binding on other judges (the concept of 'precedent'). Higher court decisions are also binding on lower courts. The hierarchy is: the House of Lords; the Court of Appeal; High Court Judges. These courts deal with both criminal law and civil law. Magistrates and Crown Courts deal mostly with criminal law only.

Some law is not well established and may never be tried . . . but it may still be the law! Some legislation may have been moulded by numerous challenges. No one is expected to know all of these – this is why there are lawyers, unions and government. However, all teachers are expected to have 'due regard' to the law, and how they might achieve this is explored within these pages.

ROLES OF THE DCSF, GTC AND TEACHING UNIONS

Government departments change names almost as often as there is a change of government. At the time of writing the government department concerned with education is the Department for Children, Schools and Families (DCSF) but it has in recent years been the DfES (Department for Education and Skills), the DfE (Department for Education), the DES (Department of Education and Science), and the DfEE (Department for Education and Employment). In this book there will be references to articles published by the government through all these department titles. More frequently nowadays the government publishes over the internet, so that often hard copies of documents are not readily available.

The General Teaching Council in England (GTCE) is a relatively new body (September 2000), although teachers have been suggesting the need for this type of independent, regulatory body, such as other professions have (an example being the Law Society for Lawyers), for many years. It has three main roles: to maintain a register of qualified teachers in England and enable professional self-regulation; to advise government and other interested parties on key issues within education; and, to act as advocates for teachers. The Teaching and Higher Education Act (1998) identified two aims 'to contribute to improving standards of teaching and the quality of learning, and to maintain and improve standards of professional conduct among teachers, in the interests of the public.' (GTC 2005). At this time not all teachers with QTS are registered, since those not teaching in maintained schools do not have to register (e.g. those teaching in Higher Education or Further Education). Full details of the GTC's work can be found at www.gtce.org.uk. Newly qualified teachers do have to register when they start work although details of their QTS will be forwarded by the DCSF to the GTC.

The strong union representation for teachers provided by the five major teaching unions (often seen by teachers as their 'professional bodies') has meant that the third aspect of the GTC's role is not yet fully established. The unions provide teachers with legal support, particularly when things 'go wrong' and continue to be the 'voice' of teachers (hence their perceived role as advocacy for teachers). They also advise government. It is imperative that all those working in education – teachers, teaching assistants and administrators – belong to a union and avail themselves of the support offered. Once an incident has occurred it may be too late to join a union.

FIVE KEY AREAS

The book explores five key areas: the statutory basis for education (Chapter 1); the curriculum and assessment (Chapter 2); equal opportunities (Chapter 3); health and safety (Chapter 4); and employment (Chapter 5).

The first key area 'sets the scene' by exploring a little of the history of education and its legal status. Aspects of attendance and discipline, home–school agreements, exclusions, corporal punishment, and complaints procedures as well as accountability issues are examined through examples of practice. There is some consideration of how to achieve 'best practice' within school policies.

Chapter 2 considers the National Curriculum, a relatively new, statutory concept in England and Wales, and its influence on teaching and learning in schools. The non-statutory guidance, including that of the national strategies, is also explored because this will enable teachers to consider how the statutory curriculum and assessment might be taught. Non-statutory guidance can support the law, but does not have to be followed. The chapter includes consideration of religious education, sex education and drugs education within the statutory curriculum. It discusses sporting achievements and the subject of charging for education within the state sector. Assessment is viewed as achievement and attainment whilst consideration is made of accountability through discussion of pupils' educational records and written reports to parents. Examples of good practice are shared and considered.

Chapter 3 considers the duty of schools to provide education without discrimination on the basis of disability, gender or ethnic background. It includes the Special Educational Needs Code of Practice and the distinction between special needs and special educational needs. This section includes information about the disapplication or modification of the National Curriculum. Vignettes of possible scenarios in the primary classroom provide material for reflection or discussion of the class teacher's approach to these situations.

The following two chapters on Health and Safety and Employment reflect upon the application of the law to schools. School security, parental access to their children's education, child protection, and data protection issues are explored. The law on employment protection, the role of governors and the head teacher, and disciplinary and competency issues are explored within performance management and appraisal. Teachers' pay and negotiation at interview are considered and recent workforce reforms including rights to preparation, planning and assessment (PPA) for the teacher are examined.

USING THIS BOOK

This book is meant to be supportive and accessible for teachers. It is quite acceptable to dip into it rather than read it from cover to cover. To support this, each chapter follows a similar pattern. Explanation of the law as it applies to schools and teachers forms the main part of the text. Marginal notes identify individual Acts and governmental circulars. Boxed vignettes describe incidents based on true events and the reader is encouraged to reflect upon these and consider their own likely response in a similar situation. Their professional experience often means that teachers don't allow situations to occur, so the reader might also consider the antecedent to the incident described and how it might have been avoided in the first place. Of course incidents do occur, and many of these have actually happened to the author or her colleagues in school. Possible responses appear at the end of each chapter. They do not always identify the full legal answer because many such situations never get to law. Such situations are much more likely to be covered by decisions of courts rather than in Acts of Parliament. At the end of the book is a bibliography and opportunity for further reading.

Being challenged about knowledge can be very 'deskilling'. In writing about this book I was challenged by a colleague about my use of language in describing the law. The discussion we had came down to the use of the word 'for'. I believe that teachers will never come to an understanding about the law and how it works if they are afraid of being challenged about the words they use. In no way is this book an 'authority' on the law. It may have words and phrases which lawyers or others in the profession will take issue with, but its focus is on understanding the law in order to develop skills, not on knowledge of the law. Please do not use this book as a complete statement of the law – it can only be an outline at best. Full professional advice should be sought in relation to any particular set of circumstances.

Consider these questions. Can you answer them? If you cannot, this book is for you.

REFLECTION

- Get a copy of your school's Home-School Agreement; read it and consider the value of it for parents/ carers and the school. Is it enforceable?
- Find out what the RE policy for your school is; is it purely a curriculum document or does it link to the school's pastoral approach?
- What do you feel is the purpose of collective worship in your school?
- How is money collected for trips in your school? What is the wording on the letter sent home to ask for voluntary contributions? If parents don't pay can their children be excluded? Is this the same for a school journey (which includes overnight stays)?
- How is reporting to parents managed in the school you are now in? How frequently does it occur? Is this often enough? What if parents don't attend?
- Are there any children who have a disability in school? How are their needs met?
- What child protection training have you already had? Look at your school's child protection policy and consider how it applies to you in your practice. What do you understand by 'safer recruitment'?

① The statutory basis for education

Teachers are employed by schools to provide education for their pupils, and many aspects of this task are governed by the law. This country spends a vast amount of money on education and there are many rules and regulations which govern its quality. There is a variety of government departments and quasi-autonomous non-governmental organisations (quangos) which provide advice and information. Teachers need to be aware of the wide range of statutory and non-statutory guidelines which govern their profession. An appropriate level of awareness is one of the pre-conditions for gaining qualified teacher status (QTS).

Within the current legislation, the Secretary of State for Children, Schools and Families has the power to make Statutory Instruments (regulations and orders) embodying more detailed legal requirements which are set out in principle in Acts of Parliament. The Department for Children, Schools and Families (DCSF) also offers guidance both on the law and on general policy, by means of circulars and administrative memoranda. The Qualifications and Standards Authority (QCA) provides extensive guidance for teachers on planning the curriculum and the standards expected from different year groups. This guidance is based on the legal requirements and is followed closely by many schools.

The importance of teacher awareness of the current legislation and non-statutory guidance is indicated by the following items, taken from recent legislation:

2002 Education Act

- From November 2002, the foundation stage became part of the National Curriculum.

2002 Education Act, Sections 34–35 and 119–148, and 2005 Education Act

- From February 2003 the new Foundation Stage Profile was introduced – a national scheme, based on observations accumulated over a period of time, of children working and playing in foundation stage settings, providing a more appropriate means of assessment of young children and replacing the former baseline assessment.
- At the same time, the role of teachers with QTS and those without was clarified.
- Guidance on how classroom assistants can be used is outlined and, with workforce reform, has been developed and changed.

Schools Standards and Framework Act 1998, Sections 1–4

- Since the start of the school year 2001/02, all infant classes should have a maximum of thirty pupils.

- Education Action Zones (EAZs) and Forums have been set up. An EAZ has wide-ranging powers: it may alter teachers' pay and conditions, for example. Appointments to the Forums are made by the governing bodies of the participating schools and the Secretary of State. The governing bodies of these schools may arrange for the Forum to discharge any of their functions. As of March 2007 there were 47 Education Action Zones, or Excellence in Cities Action Zones (1999 to 2006).
- From September 1999, all schools were allocated to a new category of school and from January 2003 there was introduced the opportunity for a new type of school to be created – the 'all age' Academies. The 2005 Education Act further categorised schools.
- In 2006 the Education and Inspections Act introduced 'Trust Schools'.
- Each maintained school must adopt a home–school agreement and associated parental declaration.
- Several relevant Statutory Instruments have recently come into force, six of which cover the School Admissions Code of Practice.
- Local Education Authorities (LEAs) will in future be known as Local Authorities (LAs).

As legislation continues there will be additions to these aspects but, importantly, the Acts that appear in the margins add to the statutory basis for education that first appeared in the 1870 Education Act. Prior to this Act, voluntary societies (often religious) had provided education for young people. The new Liberal Party legislation provided for the establishment of 'School Boards' (a term still used by some today) to fill the gaps and offer education (at a fee) in areas where there was none. These boards could apply for public money or grants to help support those not so well off, providing elementary education for children between the ages of five and ten. Each board had elected members, including (controversially) women, who oversaw the provision for elementary education in their area. Actually they only lasted for 32 years, as the next (Conservative) government abolished them in the 1902 Education Act, by handing over responsibility to newly formed Local Education Authorities, which were also given powers to establish secondary schools. Today's education system is mainly governed by four Acts which consolidate, but don't change, the statutory principles and provisions for education previously laid down. The early Acts had not established free education: this did not occur until the 1944 Education Act when the school leaving age was raised to 15. Independent schools are not regulated by Education Acts, but Local Authorities (LAs) are required to provide for education for all children of statutory age (from the term after their fifth birthday to 16 years).

Schools have been given different names over the years which usually related to the age of children being taught within them: elementary, first, middle, secondary, JMI (Junior Mixed and Infant), primary, junior, nursery and infant. Further schools for older children have been variously classed as grammar, high, county, comprehensive, central or secondary modern. These terms may still be

Schools Standards and Framework Act 1998, Sections 10–13
2005 Education Act

Education and Inspections Act 2006

Schools Standards and Framework Act 1998, Sections 110–111

The first Education Act to be established in this country was in 1870 by the Liberal MP for Bradford, William Edward Forster.

The 1902 Education Act was controversial, and it has been suggested that it may have resulted in the government losing the 1906 general election. In particular, many nonconformists campaigned against it, as people refused to pay school taxes.

The 1944 Education Act was brought to Parliament by R. A. (Rab) Butler. This left-wing Conservative MP's Act established state education.

in use but, whatever the age group of children being taught, state schools are today classed as community, voluntary aided, voluntary controlled or foundation (also termed 'trust') schools. Within these four types there are other types including a return of 'all through' age group schools within the maintained sector (academies) and 'specialist' schools (mainly within the secondary sector). In the independent sector there is a greater variety, with individual schools identifying their character, but they are often all-age schools.

School Teachers' Pay and Conditions Act 1991

If you feel the situation outlined appears complex and fraught with hidden dangers, then you are to some extent correct! Good schools are well aware of the legal requirements, and develop policies to indicate exactly what teachers must do to comply with the law. It is also most important that you consider joining a professional body which will supply the expertise, advice and resources you will need if you are unfortunate enough to find yourself in difficulties. Teachers' professional duties are set out in the current School Teachers' Pay and Conditions Document sent annually to all schools.[1]

Race Relations Act 1976; Sex Discrimination Act 1975; Health and Safety at Work Act 1974, Sections 7, 8; Children Act 1989; 1997 Education Act

The picture is one of a range of organisations whose cooperation is vital to secure the good education of all children. Teachers are part of one of these organisations and are therefore subject to aspects of the law relating to education. Teachers' legal responsibilities are found in a very wide range of legislation, and teachers need to be aware of the issues considered in legislation regarding race, equal opportunities, health and safety, children's welfare, child abuse, physical restraint of children and detention of children.

In this information-technology age government has established internet links[2] which will support teachers in guidance to the law.

THE STATUTORY BASIS FOR THE OPERATION OF SCHOOLS

1996 Education Act, Section 7; Section 19 (1); Education. . .otherwise than at school (**EOTAS**); Nursery Education and Grant Maintained Schools Act 1996; 2002 Education Act, Sections 179, 180; Education (Teachers) Regulations 1993; School Inspections Act 1996; School Standards and Framework Act 1998; Education and Inspections Act 2006

Teachers are not the only group subject to the law. All parents must send their children to school throughout the years of compulsory school age, although they may choose to educate their children at a place other than school. More recent legislation allows Ofsted (Office for Standards in Education, Children's Services and Skills) access to inspect the provision for children educated in such a way.

The head and governors must make sure that there are sufficient members of staff with suitable qualifications to secure an education appropriate to the ages, abilities, aptitudes and needs of the pupils. Each LA must ensure that there are sufficient schools providing primary and secondary education available for their area, although they are no longer required to secure provision for those over compulsory school age. The new framework for inspection of schools puts an emphasis on self-evaluation. The most recent legislation does not change this framework but expands it to include other children's services (DfES 2006d). Governing bodies of schools are required in their governance to have a strategic vision for their schools and see that it is carried out by the head teacher and senior management of the school, through receiving reports and asking questions as 'critical friends'. Schools have a structure for management that reflects the needs of their school.

2005 Education Act; Education and Inspections Act 2006

1981 Education Act; Code of Practice on SEN; 1996 Education Act; School Standards and Framework Act 1998

LAs are required in certain circumstances to carry out an assessment of children with special educational needs (SEN) and then to make and maintain a statement specifying the special provision required for each such child. If the name of a maintained school is specified in the child's statement, then the governing body of the school is required to admit the child, even where this might result in the size of the class in that school exceeding any limit set.

1996 Education Act; School Standards and Framework Act 1998; 2005 Education Act

The Secretary of State has specific responsibilities with regard to the curriculum of maintained schools, the financing of schools and the securing of teacher training opportunities within maintained schools (the quality of the teaching force). The Secretary of State has the power to intervene where LAs or governing bodies are exercising their functions under the Education Acts unreasonably, or have failed to discharge any duty under the Acts.

ATTENDANCE AND DISCIPLINE

Children have to attend school regularly to learn, they have to be taught for a recommended amount of time each week, and it is reasonable to expect them to behave during this process. Where this is not the case, parents and head teachers have legal expectations placed upon them.

Lesson hours

To support teachers, government regularly produces circulars which outline the expectations of the legislation, e.g. DES Circular 7/90

The overall number of lesson hours is not prescribed, although guidance is given. It is suggested that governing bodies of all maintained schools should take as a general guide to good practice:

- 21 hours for pupils aged 5 to 7
- 23.5 hours for pupils aged 8 to 11
- 24 hours for pupils aged 12 to 16.

The guidance goes on to suggest that secondary schools may wish to consider offering 25 hours lesson time to pupils in Key Stage 4 (14–16-year-olds). The recommended lesson hours do not include time for collective worship, registration or breaks.

The guidance for the three core subjects was that they were expected to take up 20 per cent of the curriculum each, leaving 40 per cent for the foundation subjects, but the introduction of the literacy and numeracy strategies in primary schools has meant that science (in particular) has lost this 20 per cent core status, often only appearing on the curriculum once a week. The literacy and numeracy strategies established daily lessons for literacy (not English) and mathematics (not 'numeracy') but the Primary National Strategy introduced *Excellence and Enjoyment* (DfES 2003) encouraging the 'piggybacking' of subjects in order to increase the amount of time spent on each. The debate regarding the strategies is ongoing, with the most recent advice remodelling them into *The Primary Framework for Literacy and Mathematics* (2006). Neither is statutory, although the most recent legislation will make the use of the strategy material statutory for children who are not achieving.[3]

INCIDENT 1: JEHAN	Mrs T, a parent, has been rude to two members of staff. She is not happy about discussions regarding her child working in the outside classroom in reception, feeling that now that Jehan has started school she should be doing 'real work' not play. The class teacher and teaching assistant have explained that structured play is an appropriate way of working with young children, but Mrs T wants Jehan to begin to do sums and to learn to read. Her husband is a member of the governing body, and she takes up the matter with him.

Secondary schools are only now seeing the recommendation for literacy and numeracy strategies in their curriculum (DfES 2005). A Key Stage 3 strategy was introduced in 2000 and government identifies this as the reason standards have risen in English and mathematics. The Secondary National Strategy is expected to 'build on the successes of the Key Stage 3 Strategy as the work is extended across the 11–16 range' (ibid.: 3).

Attendance: duty of parents

1996 Education Act; School Standards and Framework Act 1998

Parents must ensure that their child receives suitable full-time education, either by regular attendance at school or otherwise, from the beginning of the term after he or she attains the age of 5 until he or she has reached the age of 16.

Attendance orders and supervision orders

1996 Education Act; School Standards and Framework Act 1998; 2002 Education Act; DfEE Circular 11/99

Parents who do not send their children to school regularly may be prosecuted for failing to ensure that their child is properly educated. In such circumstances, the LA may serve a School Attendance Order or may apply to the courts for an Education Supervision Order, which puts the child under the supervision of the LA. Ofsted Inspectors are now empowered to inspect education otherwise than at school and have had their powers of entry extended.

Attendance registers

1996 Education Act; School Standards and Framework Act 1998; Data Protection Acts 1984 and 1998; SI 1995, No 2089; SI 1997, No. 2624; DfEE Circulars 7/97, 7/98, 8/98, 7/99, 8/99, 10/99, 11/99

All schools must keep an attendance register in which pupils are marked present or absent at the beginning of each morning and once during the afternoon session. Schools must distinguish in their attendance registers between authorised absences, unauthorised absences, and approved educational activity of pupils aged 5–16. They must publish rates of authorised and unauthorised absence in annual reports and absence rates in school prospectuses. Authorised absence means authorised by the parent or carer – illness, a visit to the dentist, etc. The absence must be explained in writing. Schools generally expect teachers to keep all such records and draw frequent absence to the attention of the head teacher. Schools may keep attendance and admission registers on a computer, subject to certain safeguards relating to the correction and preservation of the registers. If kept on a computer, the attendance register should be printed at least once a month. At the end of each school year these sheets must be bound into annual volumes. These, like the manual registers, must be kept securely and for three years from the last date of entry.

Education Welfare Officers (EWOs) from the LA, also known as Education Social Workers, check attendance registers on a regular basis to ensure that they are completed in accordance with the school's policy and to identify any patterns of absence not already notified. The governing body (which is legally responsible for the attendance register) must register with the Data Protection Registrar under the Data Protection Act 1998.

HOME–SCHOOL AGREEMENTS

School Standards and Framework Act 1998; Education and Inspections Act 2006

All state schools must adopt a home–school agreement. A home–school agreement is a statement explaining the school's aims and values; the school's responsibilities towards pupils of compulsory school age; the responsibilities of the pupils' parents; and what the school expects of its pupils. Teachers are in the position of implementing this, and must therefore be aware of its contents and implications for the classroom. Before adopting or revising this agreement, the governing body must consult all parents of current pupils of compulsory school age and take reasonable steps to ensure that they sign the parental declaration to indicate that they understand and accept the agreement. Many schools involve school councils in the process of refining and developing these expectations. The governing body – and the staff – must be aware of any guidance issued by the Secretary of State. A child must not be excluded from school, nor should a child and/or his parents suffer any adverse consequences, on account of a refusal to sign the parental declaration. The governing body or the LA must not:

- invite a parent or child to sign the parental declaration before the child has been admitted to the school
- make the signing of the parental declaration a condition of the child's admission to the school
- base a decision as to whether to admit a child to the school on whether his or her parents are or are not likely to sign the parental declaration.

In 2003 the Anti-social Behaviour Act identified parental responsibility in their children's behaviour through contracts. Most recently this has been extended (Education and Inspections Act 2006) 'to ensure that parents take proper responsibility for their children's behaviour at school' (DfES 2006d).

INCIDENT 2: PETER	Walking across the quad I could see Peter Bailey from year 10 and his gang talking together. As I got near them they acted as if they were hiding something. I was on my own so decided to come and get reinforcements – I think Bailey's brought in a flick-knife!

EXCLUSIONS

1996 Education Act;
School Standards and
Framework Act 1998; 2002
Education Act; Education
and Inspections Act 2006;
DES Circular 7/87; DFE
Circular 8/94; DfEE
Circulars 10/99, 11/99

The head teacher maintains discipline, taking the governors' views into account. The head teacher is solely responsible for deciding that a pupil may be excluded, either for a fixed term or permanently. He or she must inform a parent of an excluded pupil who is under 18 (or the pupil, if aged 18 or over) of the exclusion and the reasons for it, and explain that they may give their views to the governors and the LA. The governors have the right to tell the head teacher to reinstate the pupil (the LA does not have this right in cases of permanent exclusions in voluntary aided schools). In cases of permanent exclusions there is the right of formal appeal, arrangements for which must be made by the LA (or by the governors in voluntary aided schools), if the pupil has not been reinstated. In extreme cases, Paragraph 7 of schedule 1 of the 1996 Education Act provides for the teacher in charge of a pupil referral unit to exclude a pupil from the unit on disciplinary grounds (but see below concerning adjustments in the 2002 Education Act). The LA's duty to provide for education remains. Where a child's behaviour makes permanent exclusion from a pupil referral unit necessary, the LA would need to consider whether to set in hand a formal assessment of special educational needs. The 2002 Education Act makes adjustments to these existing laws on exclusions, allowing Government to respond more quickly than before to any need to change the law to reflect changing circumstances, and introduce a retrospective right of appeal for parents of pupils permanently excluded from a pupil referral unit.

Education and Inspections
Act 2006

Recent legislation has extended the role of parents of excluded children. They (the parents) are now responsible for the first five days of exclusion (whether fixed or permanent) with the governing body and eventually the LA providing alternative provision after that time.

CORPORAL PUNISHMENT

School Standards and
Framework Act 1998;
DfEE Circular 10/98

Corporal punishment is not allowed in any school.

COMPLAINTS

1996 Education Act;
School Standards and
Framework Act 1998; DES
Circular 1/89; DfEE
Circulars 7/98, 8/98

Many parents express dissatisfaction with their child's education. This may be directed at the class teacher or the head teacher. All schools must have a policy for dealing with complaints, and it is sensible for teachers to be members of a professional body which can offer advice and support in this situation. There are formal procedures for dealing with some complaints about the school – complaints about admissions, charging or the curriculum, for example. Parents – or any interested persons – can complain to the Secretary of State, if they believe that a governing body is failing to carry out its duties or is acting 'unreasonably' in using its powers. Although not a legal requirement, it is suggested that the school prospectus should contain information on the procedures for handling complaints about the curriculum.

CONCLUSION

The statutory basis for schools is contained in a number of Acts and explained in circulars regularly published by government departments. This statutory basis is unlikely to change, having been established for more than fifty years, although there are likely to be changes to the range and type of education. Children are entitled to free, state-provided education, and it is teachers' responsibility to see that this entitlement is the best available. The chapters that follow identify the legislation that governs how education in state maintained schools is realised.

RESPONSE TO INCIDENT 1: JEHAN

Parents' perceptions of how their children are taught are often influenced by the way they themselves were taught, and by the media, which still challenges education with the '3 Rs' or nostalgic suggestions that education is not as good as it once was. The first point in response to this incident is to consider the responsibility of the class teacher. Although Mrs T should not have been rude, she was within her rights to ask the class teacher and teaching assistant about her daughter's provision. Clearly Mrs T was unhappy with the reception staff response and should have gone to the head teacher. If she was still unhappy with the response then she should have followed the school's policy on complaining. All schools should have a clear policy on complaints but before this becomes a complaint, Mrs T could have been encouraged to visit and look at the teacher's lesson plans to see how children learn in the reception class. Individual records will show how Jehan is progressing and what she is learning, but these may be limited at the beginning of a term. The class teacher might have considered involving the head teacher, who could manage Mrs T away from the classroom and perhaps suggest some ways of reassuring her.

In this actual case, Mrs T did complain to her husband (a member of the governing body), who brought the matter to a committee of the governing body. The head teacher, not the governing body, is responsible for the day-to-day running of the school. No formal complaint had been made by the class teacher or the teaching assistant about Mrs T's behaviour, and the head teacher's response was that he was aware of the situation and was supporting and monitoring it. It was not an issue for the governing body, not even acting as 'critical friend'. It is impossible and inappropriate for individual governors to be involved in the day-to-day running of the school. The critical friend role involves questioning of the head teacher on the strategic overview of the school – how it is achieving children's learning. Individual incidents should not reach the governing body unless through official complaint. Mr T, as governor, may have been able to reassure his wife, or together they could talk to the head teacher (with Mr T as parent, not governor) who should have been able to reassure them too.

It is interesting to note the increasing role of governors in the management of schools, but important to recognise that the head teacher and senior management team are the day-to-day managers, and that governors can overstep the mark. However, Ofsted inspects schools on 'Leadership, Management and Governance' so the governors' role is very important. You might consider exploring the role of governors in your school. How often do you see them in school talking to a variety of people, including children as well as attending assemblies and concerts or shows? Have they visited your classroom, or talked to you in your management capacity?

RESPONSE TO INCIDENT 2: PETER	Quite rightly, this teacher did not try and tackle Peter Bailey on his own. But tackling a pupil even with reinforcements can exacerbate a situation and make it far worse. From this vignette it appears that Peter is doing no more than showing something to his friends. It would be against school regulations and the law to have a flick knife, or any potentially 'offensive' weapon. Head teachers or senior managers can confiscate weapons but whether the police are called in to 'arrest' is a different matter.
	A member of staff may search for articles he or she believes are being carried but the Violent Crime Reduction Act (2005) is quite clear on how this should be carried out. Teachers' professional bodies give clear advice too – check up now!
	The best advice is to have a senior member of staff (of the same gender as the pupil) carry out the search in the presence of another member of staff (also of the same gender) and, if possible, the pupil's parent or carer. It should be carried out only on the premises of the school, or within the schools' remit, e.g. on a school trip or school journey.
	As with any other interaction with children, teachers are expected to judge the situation in a professional way. If in their judgement the pupil has not been planning to use the knife, then the police need not be called. If the pupil is not from the school, it may be advisable not to search.
	Since the murder of Philip Lawrence, a head teacher in Maida Vale, in December 1995 schools have been more aware of how things can escalate. More children are bringing knives to school: even in primary schools. Managing these difficult situations calls on teachers' professional ability to 'read' a situation. Check what the procedures are if you suspect pupils in your school are carrying knives: know what to do before you get into the situation.
	Concerns about being challenged for assault have been addressed in the Education and Inspections 2006 Act. It clarifies the 'statutory right for school staff to discipline pupils, putting an end to the "You can't tell me what to do" culture.' (DfES 2006d: 2).

NOTES

1 http://www.teachernet.gov.uk/management/payandperformance/pay/
2 http://www.dfes.gov.uk/publications/guidanceonthelaw;
   http://www.teachernet.gov.uk
3 The Government's latest proposals establish the support material from the literacy and numeracy strategies as statutory for children not achieving.

2 The curriculum and assessment

1996 and 2005 Education
Acts; School Standards
and Framework Act 1998;
DES Circular 5/89, DFE
1/94, DFEE 2/99; QCA,
2002 *Designing and
Timetabling the Primary
Curriculum*

The school and its staff have legal responsibilities relating to the curriculum and its assessment. The basic curriculum for all schools consists of the National Curriculum, plus religious education and sex education (for pupils at secondary school and pupils of secondary school age at special schools). The amount of time that should be allocated to each subject area was discussed in Chapter 1. In addition to the subjects and aspects outlined, there are areas which must be addressed and which are inspected by Ofsted. These include pupils' spiritual, moral, social and cultural education as identified in the second aim of the school curriculum (see below and DfEE/QCA 1999) and personal, social and health education and citizenship. Other aspects of the School Curriculum include consideration regarding financial capability, enterprise education and education for sustainable development (DfEE/QCA 1999: 22, 23). The National Strategies for Literacy and Numeracy are non-statutory, but are also discussed.

In order to examine the statutory requirements, the National Curriculum will be considered first, followed by religious education and sex education. The other aspects will then follow.

THE NATIONAL CURRICULUM

1996 and 2002 Education
Acts; School Standards
and Framework Act 1998;
DfEE Circulars 7/98, 8/98,
7/99, 8/99

The National Curriculum applies to pupils of statutory school age and those in funded places in schools and pre-school provision. The curriculum of a maintained school must include the National Curriculum and religious education, and be balanced and broadly based. The Secretary of State proposed various changes to the original National Curriculum, and a revised National Curriculum was sent to schools in 1999. It took effect from September 2000 (and for citizenship education, from September 2002). In November 2002 the 'Foundation Stage' became a statutory part of this National Curriculum and the same Act (2002 Education Act) allowed changes to Key Stage 4 (to accommodate expected changes to A levels and GCSEs). It is the professional responsibility of teachers – including trainee teachers – to become familiar with the document for the National Curriculum within the relevant sector.[1]

The governing body and the head teacher must ensure that the National Curriculum is provided for all pupils and that its assessment procedures are carried out. The prospectus must contain the school's curriculum statement and information on teaching methods. As the next tier in the structure, teachers must deliver what is described in their school's prospectus.

The National Curriculum consists of the core subjects (English, mathematics, and science) and the foundation subjects: information and communication technology (sometimes included with the core subjects, to form 'the extended core'), design and technology, physical education, history, geography, art and design, and music. At Key Stage 3, citizenship and a modern foreign language (MFL) are added although MFL is no longer statutory at Key Stage 4. Subjects are arranged in Programmes of Study, and each National Curriculum subject is implemented by a Statutory Order (National Curriculum Order), which is statutory. From 2010 a modern foreign language will be added to the foundation subjects in primary schools. In Wales, in schools where all teaching is in Welsh, Welsh is a core subject and English is a foundation subject. In schools where the teaching language medium is English, Welsh is a foundation subject.

INCIDENT 3: RICKY	A parent comes to see you one morning, concerned about his son Ricky, who is very reluctant to come to school. He asks if you will keep him with you during playtimes and lunchtimes, as Ricky is particularly afraid of the playground.

RELIGIOUS EDUCATION

1996 Education Act; School Standards and Framework Act 1998; DFE Circular 1/94

Schools must teach religious education (RE) in accordance with a locally agreed syllabus. The locally agreed syllabus is drawn up by the LA in consultation with its Standing Advisory Council on Religious Education (SACRE). Special schools may use the agreed syllabus (as far as possible) but this is not a legal requirement. In foundation or voluntary controlled schools with a religious character, the syllabus is the responsibility of the foundation governors. Parents have the right to withdraw their child from all or part of RE.

In 2006 QCA developed a national non-statutory framework for RE, aimed primarily at local decision makers who have responsibility for provision within maintained schools in England such as LAs, ASCs (Agreed Syllabus Conferences) and SACREs. It identifies two major learning objectives of RE:

• Learning about religion
• Learning from religion.

Further information is available on the internet.[2]

The Ofsted report on RE in schools in its Annual Report (2004/05) identified that schools needed to continue developing RE, particularly to support children's spiritual, moral, social and cultural development. Importantly Ofsted recognise that where both learning objectives are achieved, children are able to extend learning from knowledge to application of that knowledge, so making it more relevant to their own lives.

SEX EDUCATION

1996 Education Act; School Standards and Framework Act 1998; DFE Circular 5/94

The governing body is responsible for deciding whether sex education should be included in the curriculum. Teachers in that school must follow the decision made by the governors, which may be to not have a sex education programme. Governors have to keep a record of their decision and of their policy, and teachers must deliver the content and organise this part of the curriculum. Documents must be available to interested parties (parents, LA officials, inspectors). The legislation states that any sex education which schools provide should encourage pupils to develop a regard for moral considerations and the value of family life. Parents have the right to withdraw pupils from part or all of the sex education provided by the school, unless it forms part of the National Curriculum. (In science, teaching may include reproduction, new life, growth and so on. Such topics may include aspects of sex education and are compulsory. They should be covered by the governors' policy.)

PUPILS' SPIRITUAL, MORAL, SOCIAL AND CULTURAL DEVELOPMENT

1996 Education Act

The curriculum of a state school must promote the spiritual, moral, cultural, mental and physical development of pupils and of society, and prepare pupils for the opportunities, responsibilities and experiences of adult life.

There are areas in addition to the National Curriculum which the law insists that pupils study. Guidance at the beginning of the National Curriculum documentation identifies the values, aims and purposes which make links between the curriculum that a school develops and the National Curriculum, which is seen as 'an important element of the school curriculum' (DfEE/QCA 1999: 10). This same document (Ibid.: 11) identifies two aims of any school curriculum:

1. The school curriculum should aim to provide opportunities for all pupils to learn and to achieve.
2. The school curriculum should aim to promote pupils' spiritual, moral, social and cultural development and prepare all pupils for the opportunities, responsibilities and experiences of life.

It is these two aims that identify aspects that the head teacher and governors need to consider when developing the school curriculum – inclusion and spiritual, moral, social and cultural development. In law religious education must also be taught, but is a separate aspect.

Collective worship

School Standards and Framework Act 1998; 2005 Education Act, Section 45

All schools must provide for all pupils to attend a daily act of collective worship, which over a term must be broadly Christian in character. This should normally occur on the school premises, with the exception of special occasions which may take place elsewhere, if appropriate consultation has taken place with the head teacher. Teachers are usually expected to lead acts of collective worship, and must be aware of the requirements. There may be a school timetable of topics to be covered; the act of collective worship may relate closely to the syllabus for RE; some assemblies may be held in class. Teachers are usually expected to contribute to the records that must be kept of content. Special schools should organise daily collective worship so far as is practicable. In community or foundation schools without a religious character, the arrangements for collective worship are made by the head teacher in consultation with the governing body. In foundation schools with a religious character or voluntary schools,[3] the arrangements for collective worship are made by the governing body after consulting with the head teacher. In these schools the inspection of collective worship is covered in the separate inspection of religious education. Parents have the right to withdraw their child from all or part of collective worship. Teachers are responsible for arranging the safe supervision of such children. The head teacher may apply to the SACRE for a ruling that the requirement for Christian collective worship should not apply. Inspection of collective worship is commented on in annual reports from Ofsted.

PERSONAL, SOCIAL AND HEALTH EDUCATION, AND CITIZENSHIP

1996 and 2002 Education Acts

The National Curriculum handbook for primary teachers in England identifies guidance for PSHE and Citizenship – this is non-statutory. It is recognised that schools should provide health education, including education about drug misuse. Statutory aspects can be found within individual orders for Science (under Health and Safety) and PE (under Fitness and Health). It is recognised that opportunity for discussion will occur across the National Curriculum subjects. At the Foundation Stage, personal, social and emotional development is one of the six areas of learning, and now statutory. At Key Stage 3, Citizenship is a statutory area of the curriculum.

INCIDENT 4: KENNEDY

It is 3.45 and Kennedy (Year 3 – age 7) arrives back at the classroom door. 'What's the matter, Kennedy?' asks the class teacher.

'I can't find my coat,' replies Kennedy.

'Where did you leave it?'

'Here, on my peg. It's my new one – mum will kill me!'

'No she won't! She'll be angry, but let's look.'

After a search, a similar coat is found. 'That's George's, not mine,' declares Kennedy. Mum arrives in the classroom. 'Well, have you found it? I paid good money for that f***ing coat, and you're not leaving until you find it. Good bye!'

With that, she leaves the school – and Kennedy. He has lost his composure and is weeping.

Drugs education

DfES Circular 92/2004

Schools are advised to have clear policies and procedures in place for dealing with drug-related incidents on school premises and for working with other services concerned with young people to offer appropriate advice and support. Clearly, it is the teachers who are actually in the situation of delivering the policies and policing them. A very good awareness of school policies and practices is therefore vital. In 2004 the DfES provided guidance for schools which sets out the school's role in relation to all drug matters. It reiterates the point that all schools should have a drugs policy, although this is not statutory, and the only statutory aspect of drugs education is within the statutory guidance for science orders.

SPORTING ACHIEVEMENTS

Teachers are not required to provide after-school clubs for sport, or supervise matches, but this is an area that many schools and most parents prize highly. It is not a legal requirement, but schools usually include a statement in the school

Education (School Information) (England) Regulations 1996; DfEE Circulars 7/98, 8/98, 7/99, 8/99

prospectus on the school's sporting aims and provision of sport, and provide information annually on whether the school's sporting aims have been met and details of any notable sporting achievements. This presupposes teachers' awareness and voluntary participation.

THE NATIONAL STRATEGIES

2005 Education Act; Education and Inspections Act 2006; DfES: Primary National Strategy; DfES: Secondary National Strategy

At this time (2007) government has developed its National Strategies which aim to

> transform the quality of learning and teaching to benefit all children and young people in all phases and settings . . . achieved through an evidence-based focus on good practice . . . supported through national and local initiatives designed to harness the energy of our best education leaders.
>
> (DfES 2006b, Section 1.1)

The Primary National Strategy combines aspects of the Literacy Strategy and the Numeracy Strategy which have never been statutory requirements, although many schools have regarded them as such. It is expected that head teachers and governors demonstrate how their schools support children's development in literacy and numeracy, and although government offers guidance through its Primary National Strategy (originally published as *A National Strategy for Primary Schools, Excellence and Enjoyment* in 2003) these guidelines are non-statutory. However, in the 2005 Education Act, aspects of provision were made statutory where children were identified as not achieving or reaching the expected levels of attainment. Then a statutory duty is placed on head teachers and governing bodies to use the supplementary materials for literacy and numeracy (Mathematics in the new guidelines) to support children's development.

Secondary schools are subjected to similar guidance from government (DfES 2005). Discussions have included changing GCSE and Advanced-level coursework acceptance for examination; provision for other types of education such as vocational routes to employment, etc. The curriculum in Key Stage 3 covers twelve subject areas, adding modern foreign languages and citizenship to the primary curriculum (July 2007) as well as RE, sex and relationship education, and careers advice. Support for teachers in providing this wide curriculum is given within the Key Stage 3 National Strategy, which identified four principles to teaching in secondary schools: Expectations, Progression, Engagement and Transformations. Like the development of the Primary National Strategy the Secondary National Strategy has undergone reforms following various pilots. Ofsted clearly monitors provision (e.g. its update on the condensed curriculum (DfESe 2006).

The National Curriculum for 16–19-year-olds is further amended to providing the core (English, mathematics and science) and other foundation subjects (ICT, PE and citizenship) and work-related learning. Pupils can also elect to study other subjects (such as foundation subjects of the National Curriculum studied at earlier key stages). In the Education and Inspections Act 2006 reform to the 14–19 curriculum includes the introduction of 14 new specialised diplomas, which are being developed by employers (DCSF 2007), the first of which will come on line in September 2008. Although the working group on the 14–19 curriculum chaired by Mike Tomlinson (DfES 2004) originally envisaged that diplomas would replace and expand the GCSE and A-level provision, government has decided to keep the established academic qualifications (although reform in terms of examination and course work is likely).

CHARGING

1996 Education Act; DES Circular 2/89

Charging for admission and education in all state schools is prohibited. There are some exceptions: for example, tuition of individual pupils, or pupils in a group of up to four, to play a musical instrument (if such teaching is not an essential part of the National Curriculum); board and lodging on a residential visit; and education provided wholly or mainly out of school hours. Governing bodies must draw up a charging policy.

ASSESSMENT

Education Acts 1996 and 2002; School Standards and Framework Act 1998; DFE 1994, *Code of Practice on the Identification and Assessment of Special Educational Needs*; DfES 2001, *Special Educational Needs Code of Practice*

Schools are required to assess pupils in National Curriculum subjects at or near the end of each key stage and develop a profile of observations during the foundation stage to find out what pupils have achieved in relation to attainment targets and early learning goals for that stage of learning. Schools must also have assessment arrangements in place for identifying pupils with special educational needs, reflecting the guidance in the SEN Code of Practice. Once again, teachers must be aware of how such requirements are to be met, and carry out the procedures.

The school's results and achievements

1996 Education Act; School Standards and Framework Act 1998; Statutory Instrument 1994/1420; DfEE Circulars 7/97, 7/98, 8/98, 7/99, 8/99

Schools must make available the results of pupils' achievements in public examinations (secondary schools) and the school and national results of the National Curriculum assessments in the core subjects of English, mathematics and science of 7- and 11-year-olds (primary schools) and 14-year-olds (secondary schools). This information must be published in the school's prospectus and through other public reporting media, e.g. schools' websites, Ofsted reports, within the Self Evaluation Forms, etc.

Information about school performance

1996 and 2005 Education Acts; School Standards and Framework Act 1998; Statutory Instrument 1994/1420 and 1421; DfEE Circulars 6/98, 7/98, 8/98, 7/99, 8/99

General information about the school and specified information about school performance must be provided by head teachers to governing bodies and by governing bodies to the Secretary of State. Information will be included in the school profile which governors have to provide annually and is often used to support the marketing of the school through the school prospectus.

Pupils' educational records

Statutory Instrument 2000 (Education: School Records) Regulations (1989); Data Protection Acts 1984 and 1998

Schools – and therefore teachers – are required to keep records on every pupil, including material on academic achievements, other skills and abilities and progress in school, and must update this material at least once a year. How the records should be kept, or detailed requirements as to content, are not prescribed. There is useful guidance from the internet,[5] and schools have begun to develop comprehensive procedures, often linked to the requirements of the LA annual targets. Parents have access to pupils' records. Assessment results may be disclosed to another school only after a pupil has been admitted to that school. Importantly, ongoing assessment should inform learning. To support this aim, government has developed its Assessment for Learning (AfL) programme.[6]

Assessment records may be used in courts of law as evidence to support cases, particularly where parents may need support in asking for a Statement of Special Educational Need (see Chapter 3). Similarly, individual teachers may need assessment records to demonstrate their competence, either if a complaint case has been brought against them, or more positively if they are applying for Advanced Skills Teacher or Excellent Teacher status (see Chapter 5).

Annual written reports to parents: pupils' achievements

Statutory Instrument 1997/1368 Education (Individual Pupils' Achievements) (Information) Regulations 1997

Schools and, in practice, teachers must provide an annual written report to the parents of each pupil. The report must contain brief details of the pupil's progress in all subjects and activities covered as part of the school curriculum; details of the pupil's general progress; information on performance in all National Curriculum assessments and in public examinations; school and national comparative information about National Curriculum assessments and public examinations; an attendance record and details of the arrangements under which the report may be discussed with teachers at the school. Note that this requires a judgement of individual progress to be made in each specified area: a description of work covered by the class as a whole is not permitted. Many teachers may use the widely available software to produce reports, as the judgements made will reflect language from the National Curriculum levels (1 to 8) outlined in the relevant documents. In primary schools the focus is on levels 1 to 5 (in most cases) and these are described at the back of the National Curriculum handbooks for teachers.

CONCLUSION

In considering the curriculum and assessment, this chapter has identified the statutory aspects: the National Curriculum and RE which schools need to consider within their school curriculum. The National Strategies are not statutory, although schools must be clear about how they support children's development in literacy and mathematics. All teachers know assessment is important, but the ongoing, everyday aspects are not covered in law. The reporting of children's attainment and achievement is a statutory requirement of head teachers and governing bodies.

RESPONSE TO INCIDENT 3: RICKY	It is not the duty of the teacher to keep Ricky separated from the other children at break times. However as a responsible teacher, you would probably want to agree some means of gradually helping Ricky to lose his fears. His father's visit provides an ideal opportunity to discuss with him a joint plan, aimed at helping Ricky. All staff should know of Ricky's worries. Ricky needs to know about the plan to help him.
	Consider what strategies you could use to help integrate Ricky back into the playground. These could include 'buddying', and staying with him for a short while. You might try to develop a plan for Ricky's reintegration into the playground, identifying those strategies particularly linked to school policies. Would your reaction be different, depending on Ricky's age?
	It is unlikely that a situation such as Ricky's described above would reach the courts. The school might intervene and head teacher and perhaps Chair of Governors discuss with Ricky's parents his needs. Sometimes parents do not feel the situation has been resolved and may remove a child from school, but they would not have recourse to the law and be able to sue the school for negligence if teachers had done all that was reasonable and carried out their duty of care 'in loco parentis'

RESPONSE TO INCIDENT 4: KENNEDY	Anger is a strong emotion. Children need support in developing their own emotions, and Kennedy is learning from the situation. How the class teacher manages the situation may add to the effect. Kennedy's mum has left him at school and has, in effect, neglected him. Allowing time for her to 'cool down' is important and in this actual incident she did return twenty minutes later to collect him – without being prompted or even called. If she hadn't returned, social services would have to be called and the child might have been taken into emergency care. At one level this seems harsh, but it is where the legal requirement lies. By calming Kennedy down, and allowing his mum time to rethink her action, the class teacher can help Kennedy understand that anger is acceptable, and how we deal with it is important.
	It would not have been appropriate to wait a bit and then drive, or walk, Kennedy home. His mum knew where he was and he was safe. Teachers should not set themselves up for accusation. Being alone with a child – particularly in a car away from others – is not appropriate for a teacher.

What were your responses to these incidents? Have you had similar incidents that you now know how to respond to? In considering Incident 4 you might reflect on the suggested response. In this actual case, Kennedy's mum returned and Kennedy went home. He retrieved his coat the next day. But, a different scenario could have occurred: Kennedy could have accused the teacher of some inappropriate behaviour and by not contacting social services earlier she has put herself in a potentially difficult position. Today, accusations regarding child protection mean a teacher may be suspended from duty whilst the issue is being investigated and would include a note, even if exonerated, which would appear on any subsequent Criminal Record Bureau (CRB) enhanced check. It is clear that every action teachers take can mean they are potentially vulnerable in the law.

NOTES

1   At this time the Training and Development Agency is formulating standards for all teachers which will be applied from the beginning of their initial teacher training or education throughout their career. Details can be found at http://www.tda.gov.uk/teachers/professionalstandards.aspx

2   http://www.reonline.org.uk/ and on the Standards website at www.standards.dfes.gov.uk/schemes2/religion/teaching?view=get

3   These schools are listed within Statutory Instrument 1999 No. 2432 The Designation of Schools Having a Religious Character (England) Order 1999.

4   See also http://cowo.culham.ac.uk/guidance/

5   Try QCA www.qca.org.uk or DfES www.dfes.gov.uk or teachernet www.teachernet.gov.uk and type 'assessment' in their search boxes.

6   http://www.qca.org.uk/7659.html

3 Equal opportunities

Race Relations Act 1976; Race Relations (Amendment) Act 2000; Sex Discrimination Act 1975; School Standards and Framework Act 1998; Disability Discrimination Act 1995; Employment Equality (Religion or Belief) Regulations 2003; Statutory Instrument 2003/1660

Schools and teachers have a general duty to ensure that facilities for education are provided without discrimination on the basis of disability, gender or ethnic background. Schools must pay full regard to pupils' age, gender, ethnic background, aptitude and any special educational needs. Schools are encouraged to keep a written statement of their policy on equal opportunities. They are required to have a written race equality policy. Often schools have just one policy on equal opportunities, although the race equality aspect of this policy is a legal requirement. This should cover both staff and pupils and should be a statement of how the school intends to prevent racial discrimination, promote equality of opportunity and promote good race relations across all areas of school activity. There should be no discrimination against any pupil or member of staff on the grounds of race, sex, disability, sexual orientation, religion or belief.[1]

Schools should have a 'Race incidents' book, where instances of racist behaviour are recorded, along with the action taken. Support for understanding what a racist incident is can be sought from the Commission for Racial Equality on their website.[2]

INCIDENT 5: SHARON	It is the beginning of the school year, and the head teacher has asked that all teachers apply the 'no jewellery' school rule. Over a period of time the wearing of jewellery stops in your class, except for Sharon. The rules are that, the first time, the child is told off and removes the jewellery. If this continues and jewellery is removed more than three times, the jewellery is kept by office staff, and parents/carers are asked to come in and collect it. This has happened twice for Sharon, and on the third time her mother arrives at your door, shouting at you to stop picking on her daughter. You outline the rule, but she points out to you that lots of children in the school are wearing jewellery – albeit not in your class.

There should be no discrimination, either direct or indirect, in:

- providing teaching or allocating pupils to teaching groups
- excluding pupils
- applying standards of behaviour, dress and appearance
- giving careers guidance and work experience
- allocating resources and providing other facilities and services.

From 1997 onwards, schools were required to include in their governors' annual report:

- a description of their arrangements for admitting disabled pupils
- details of the steps they have taken to prevent pupils with disabilities from being treated less favourably than other pupils
- details of facilities provided to assist access to the school, both physically (e.g. to buildings) and to education provision (e.g. to the curriculum) by pupils with disabilities.

Now that there is no requirement to produce an annual report, this information should appear in the prospectus. These requirements do not apply to special schools. Schools themselves need to consider equal opportunities in relation to all who work there – pupils and staff.

SPECIAL EDUCATIONAL NEEDS

1996 Education Act; School Standards and Framework Act 1998; Code of Practice on the Identification and Assessment of Special Educational Needs (DFE 1994); DfES 2001, *Special Educational Needs Code of Practice*; Disability Discrimination Acts 1995 and 2005

All schools must implement the Code of Practice on the Identification and Assessment of Special Educational Needs. All teachers and beginning teachers have a professional responsibility to be aware of their duties and responsibilities under the Code of Practice. The governing body and the head teacher, and therefore also the teachers, must follow the SEN Code of Practice. The governors and the head teacher determine the school's SEN policy, publish the policy in the school prospectus and inform parents about the success of the policy through the normal processes (e.g. the school profile).

The governing body must oversee SEN, and set up appropriate staffing and funding arrangements. They must also designate a 'responsible person' to ensure that where a pupil has special educational needs, those needs are made known to all who are likely to teach that pupil. This person is often the head teacher, although many governing bodies also appoint a named governor to monitor provision. The SEN Code of Practice suggests that schools should keep a register of all pupils with SEN through a special educational needs coordinator (SENCO), and have stages of provision and review that will ensure that pupils with SEN receive appropriate attention. Where a child has been assessed as needing special education provision determined by a statement, the LA must make and maintain a statement of the special educational needs of that child, and review it annually ('annual review of a statement of special educational needs'). All staff who teach children with statements are required to contribute to the annual review of such pupils. Many of the foregoing duties are delegated to the class teacher in primary schools and subject teachers and form teachers in secondary schools. All involved in teaching the child must be aware of what is expected.

Importantly, children who have English as an Additional Language (EAL) are not considered within this provision. The 1996 Education Act is very clear about this, although children with EAL and those identified within the SEN Code of Practice are often grouped together by teachers. The 1994 Code of Practice identified stages, but these were repealed by the 2001 Code of Practice which recognises processes rather than stages. Therefore a child may be considered at 'School Action Plus' when extra provision or consultation is made.

Parents must always be part of this process, and it can be a delicate balance considering the needs of the child, parents, teachers and school staff and the other children in the school.

INCIDENT 6: BEN (PART 1)	'The first thing was I got a letter from the head teacher asking me to come and talk to her about my son, Ben . . . He's six. I went there and she said she thought he should be seen by a psychiatrist because of his behaviour. I asked her what was wrong, and she said Ben had been hitting other children in the playground, and some parents had been up to school to complain. I said my son wasn't going to be seen by a psychiatrist. He wasn't going to be sent to a special school.'
	She said, 'No, he won't be sent to a special school. But he might need to go for treatment one or two afternoons a week.' I said, 'What treatment! He's only six. He's no trouble at home. I've had no complaints about his work in class.'
	'No', she said, 'He's all right in class. It's when he gets into the playground'. I said, 'But, isn't there a grown-up in the playground to keep an eye on the children?' and she said, 'Yes, but you can't expect the helpers to spend all their time watching your son.'
	'Can't you punish him in some way? Make him miss his sports, or keep him at playtimes – in your office?', I suggested. 'I'm far too busy to have him in my office all the time', she said. I said, 'I don't mean *all* the time, I mean to punish him when he hits someone. Just now and then.'
	'No', she said, 'I recommend that the psychiatrist or educational psychologist sees Ben. I'm going to make an appointment. Now, when would it be convenient for you to take him?' 'I'm not taking him', I said. 'Can't you even look after six year olds and keep them out of trouble?' I left the school very angry.'

DISABILITIES

Disability Discrimination Acts 1995 and 2005; 1993 and 1996 Education Acts

The Disability Discrimination Act 1995 places a duty upon schools to include specific information about disabled pupils in their annual reports. This legislation took effect in schools from January 1997; the provisions do not apply to special schools.[3] Its purpose is to ensure provision for all pupils with special educational needs, including disabled pupils, with an education and school place that matches their needs. Schools must continue to publish their special educational needs policy and, of course, teachers must be aware of this as part of their professional duties. The policy should be readily available to parents, and the school prospectus must include a summary of the policy. Often, children with special educational needs will not be disabled within the meaning of the Disability Discrimination Act (DDA). However, a significant proportion of those who are disabled will have special educational needs. A special need does not necessarily mean a special educational need, but it is easy to presume it.

INCIDENT 7: EMILY	Emily had been achieving well at school, and presented as a happy confident child until she joined Year 2. She had a group of friends she played with regularly at playtimes. She then had a series of chest infections that left her needing to use an inhaler regularly. Her condition prevented her from taking part in outdoor playtimes and limited her PE sessions for a significant part of the winter. Emily's family requested that work be sent home when she was ill, but the work has not been completed.

Local authorities have a duty to place children with identified special educational needs in mainstream schools if their parents wish, and if the placement is appropriate to the child's needs, does not conflict with the interests of other children in the school and is an efficient use of the LA's resources. Governing bodies, and therefore teachers, must ensure that pupils with special needs join in everyday activities with other pupils. This can be quite a challenge for the teacher although there is support from LAs and through the SENCO.

The DDA also includes provisions covering employment, access to goods, facilities and services, and public transport. The employment provisions, which took effect in December 1996, place specific duties on governing bodies as employers. Education provided at a school is excluded from the goods and services provisions of the Act.

In 2005 the DDA introduced a Disability Equality Duty which required schools to be more proactive in their approach to promoting disability equality. Since then, schools have had to revisit plans to support their admissions. This can be a major problem in the inner cities where Victorian-built schools may spread over three or even four floors. For many governing bodies, the cost of putting in a lift shaft is beyond their annual budget, but may not be beyond their future (three-year) budget. Moving classes around or working within a cluster of schools, one of which will be able to cope more easily, can be part of the thinking. Of course, this thinking would have to become active if a child using a wheelchair applied to the school. The Government offers up-to-date advice for head teachers, class teachers and governors on their various websites.[4]

DISAPPLICATION OR MODIFICATION OF THE NATIONAL CURRICULUM
1996 and 2002 Education Acts; School Standards and Framework Act 1998

All pupils in maintained schools should follow the National Curriculum as far as possible, but it may be disapplied or modified for pupils with statements of special educational needs. The head teacher may decide the National Curriculum shall not apply, or shall apply with modifications, to a pupil without a statement for a maximum period of six months. The head teacher may also revoke or vary a direction, but may not extend its operative period. Prescribed information must be given by the head teacher to governors, the LA and the pupil's parents.

Since 2002 and the extension of the National Curriculum to include the Foundation Stage, it is less likely to be necessary for head teachers to apply for disapplication, as children can be working on a curriculum before or after their appropriate key stage. Reasons for temporary disapplication are usually linked to individual needs, and include such aspects as a child first arriving in the country and needing time to develop linguistic skills, or children who move regularly from school to school. This process has been used mainly for assessment purposes but recent amendments have made clear when it can apply. Most children in school can access the National Curriculum at an appropriate level, with P levels being introduced for those working below Level 1. Disapplication from assessment only is not appropriate either.

Parents cannot apply for children to be disapplied for religious reasons from any part of the National Curriculum and head teachers have a duty to manage the curriculum so as to include all children.

INCIDENT 8: KAMALA	A letter arrives on your desk on the first morning of term from Kamla's dad. It asks you to excuse Kamla from swimming lessons for the term 'because she has always been very nervous around water'. *(Bear in mind that there may well be socio-cultural implications in this case.)*

RESPONSE TO INCIDENT 5: SHARON	This is another case of communication breaking down. This time, it is not between the parent and class teacher, but between the teacher and her colleagues in the school. In this incident the class teacher actually referred Sharon's mother back to the head teacher who is ultimately responsible for the school rules. The mother (and Sharon) were quite correct – the school was not seeing that the rule was enforced equally, so in many respects it was going against its own equal opportunities policy. It highlights the importance of all members of staff having ownership of policies. You might consider how your school makes sure that this happens when new staff are appointed. In this case the head teacher reminded colleagues that this was the rule, and it was enforced for a while again. But, as so many members of staff did not have ownership, or thought the rule inappropriate, there came a time when the rule was not being applied once again. School rules are often there for a reason, but the more rules the school has the less able it becomes to enforce them. Some schools have a statement of vision, or a mission statement, and avoid absolute rules which cannot easily be managed. Children, whether in their classes, forms or through School Councils, should be involved in considering what the mission statement means and how it can be realised. Perhaps staff should too! The following year, Sharon was in a different class and took to wearing her jewellery again. Her new class teacher did not apply the school rule. Her previous class teacher was unable to change colleagues' approaches to school rules – the rules were all still there, but they were just not applied. She left.

CONCLUSION

There are not many areas which cause as much concern to teachers as equal opportunities. Most teachers are aware that they should not show discrimination, although as individuals they bring their own prejudices to any situation. Being 'politically correct' means there can be anxiety in not hurting people's feelings, so not addressing issues and eventually not being inclusive. Communication is an important professional skill for teachers. This includes communication with parents, children, colleagues and the wider community. Part of this communication includes trust so that teachers can accept challenge from colleagues and children. This can build individual teacher confidence so that if a teacher is challenged for a remark that could be found offensive the professional takes control, the rebuff is accepted and parties move on. This is an important aspect of professional development and one that is continuous. In reflecting on it, consider what might be an appropriate response, particularly to the incident involving Michael in Chapter 4 (Incident 11): does this become a reportable 'racist incident'?

Equality of opportunity is everyone's right, but communication is vital for it to be achievable.

INCIDENT 6: BEN (PART 2)

Ben's mother continued to refuse permission for him to see a psychiatrist. No more was heard from the school and no more reports of misbehaviour were forthcoming from the school. 'Two days later I got a letter from the head teacher, telling me the date and the time that had been fixed up for me to take my son to the psychiatrist.

'I went to the Citizens Advice Bureau to see if the head teacher could make me do that. They told me to ring the Advisory Centre for Education. I talked to someone on the phone and explained the situation. The person advised me to go straight to the school, to explain that I did not want Ben to be examined and to suggest some helpful things to the head teacher.

'I went to the school. I said, 'Look, I explained that I did not want Ben to see a psychiatrist. I'll come to school and help if you want. I don't work afternoons. He can miss a week's playtime in the afternoons, when he's naughty. I'll sit with him in the classroom while he does work. I'll warn him about it if you like.' 'No', the head teacher said, 'We can't have parents coming into school for reasons like that.' 'Well, tell me the parents who have complained about him. I'll go and talk to them.' She wouldn't tell me their names. She said again that she wanted Ben to have treatment, and that she was going to fix another appointment for a test. 'If you refuse to take him this time, I'm afraid I shall have no choice but to ask you to remove him from my school.'

'I got more advice. I wrote to the head teacher, saying that I would not accept that my son needed to see a psychiatrist, educational or any other kind. If that meant that she would stop him from going to her school, then I asked her to put that in writing to me in a letter, so that I could go to the

Education Office with the letter and get their advice on just what school they thought he could go to, if he couldn't stay where he was.

'I got no reply to that letter. She didn't write to me, and I have heard no more about it since. As far as I know Ben has not been getting into trouble.'

RESPONSE

Of course no head teacher is in a position to insist that a child sees a psychiatrist, and no psychiatrist would see a child without parental consent. At some point the head teacher might make the decision that the child's behaviour is a health and safety issue, and for this reason the child might be excluded. Discussions should be sought with the parents and LA on how the child's education can continue. Challenging the parents does not always lead to supporting a child's needs, and it is the child, and other children in school, whose education is paramount, not the parents. Their wishes are important, and opportunity for professional communication must be found, sometimes with support from the LA.

RESPONSE TO INCIDENT 7: EMILY

In considering Emily's access to PE there would be no general disapplication, because illness or holidays are not covered, so the amount of PE Emily receives must be monitored and provision arranged so that Emily can learn. Because of her special need (not a special educational need) she may require to work at different level for PE for a period of time, for example Emily could be involved in observing and evaluating other children's work. Whilst this does not replace the physical development Emily is missing, it will help her continue accessing the concepts and ideas being explored in the PE lessons she is excluded from.

What is of greater concern is her illness, absence from school and non-completion of the work supplied by the school. Here is a case where the establishment of communication with parents is necessary. The class teacher should be the first point of contact with parents, and often children in the class or Emily's friends will relay information (although it is not advisable to listen to gossip or make assumptions based on hearsay). Discussions with parents on how the school can support Emily and consideration of her needs during this period of illness will take time and require professional sensitivity. Emily may need a different type of provision (all too often we send closed worksheets home) and discussion with parents, who will have to see that Emily completes the work, may help in deciding what to send home. Using other children to support can also help.

RESPONSE TO INCIDENT 8: KAMALA	If the parent absolutely refuses to let Kamla swim, there is nothing that the teacher can do, though, of course, gentle persuasion would be recommended! As there appeared to be no medical grounds for not swimming, the teacher felt it was her duty to teach Kamla to swim. This was explained in detail to her parents, but they still objected. The teacher then wondered if the religious beliefs of the family were involved. She tactfully enquired what Kamla did during ballet lessons and was told that she wore leggings. She suggested that Kamla might swim with leggings on. Both Kamla and her parents received this suggestion with enthusiasm, and swimming remained an integral part of her curriculum.
	Since the National Curriculum, swimming has been a statutory part of Key Stage 2 provision. The school has a duty to manage the curriculum so that Kamla can take part, and this is what the teacher has done.

NOTES

1 The Training and Development Agency has formulated standards for all teachers which will be applied from the beginning of their initial teacher training or education throughout their career. Details can be found at http://www.tda.gov.uk/teachers/professionalstandards.aspx

2 Schools which have a religious character are permitted to recruit pupils and staff who are of that faith group, but they must publish their criteria and details of how these criteria will be applied.

3 www.cre.gov.uk

4 A 'special school' is one that is established to educate children with specified special needs. It can be under LA control or an independent school.

5 www.governet.gov.uk; www.teachernet.gov.uk; www.dfes.gov.uk; www.qca.org.uk

4 Health and safety

There are many Acts covering health and safety at work and in public environments. These include regulations covering electricity, noise, reporting of injuries, control of dangerous goods and environmental health issues. The 1996 Education Act and the School Standards and Framework Act 1998 also refer to particular health and safety issues in schools.

Everyone has an important role to play in health and safety. Schools must take reasonable steps to make sure that buildings, equipment and materials are safe and do not put health at risk. This applies to all who work there – pupils and staff.

The governing body should make sure that there are procedures for carrying out the required health and safety policies. The safety of adults is generally overseen by a member of staff, often either the Premises Officer (caretaker) or a senior teacher (often a union representative). The safety of children is down to individual teachers, but the head teacher has final responsibility, and it is up to the head teacher to make sure that the health and safety policies are being monitored.

IN THE CLASSROOM

There are different levels of health and safety. It is generally expected that the classroom is set up as a safe environment for learning, with the acceptable risks that can happen through learning. Different subject areas will have different risks associated with them, and it is expected that teachers will have subject knowledge that includes an understanding of risk factors. The former standards for qualified teacher status were clear that teachers should plan for 'safe and effective organ-isation' of resources, and manage them 'safely and effectively' and that children should feel 'safe and secure' in their learning environment (DfES 2002, Standards 3.1.3, 3.3.1, 3.3.8). The new standards (TDA 2007a and TDA 2007b) are more succinct and shift the responsibility for teachers being 'aware of current legal requirements and policy concerning the well-being of children and young people' (Q21; C22) so that they should 'establish a purposeful and safe learning envi-ronment' (Q30). These two 'Q' standards are extended following induction and a post-threshold teacher will be expected to have sufficient depth of knowledge to give advice on children's well-being (P6). The current documentation outlining these new standards (TDA 2007) suggests that 'sufficient depth' is dependent on the level at which teachers are working and will be evaluated through performance management (TDA, 2007c). There are now five levels: Q – Qualified; C – Core which underpins all other levels and teachers are expected to have met at the end of their Induction period; P – Post Threshold; E – Excellent Teacher, and; A – Advanced Skills Teacher. Guidance is becoming available for these levels. The most recent (Bubb 2007) offers advice not just for teachers but for those mentoring them.

A commonsense approach to health and safety suggests that any teacher is able to ensure a safe classroom environment, but recognises that accidents do happen.

INCIDENT 9: NIAMH	The first thing I [Year 2 class teacher] knew about it was when I heard a scream. I turned around and there was Niamh clutching her hand. Rosaleen was looking shocked. 'I didn't do anything,' she said. It seems Niamh had been standing at the quiet room door looking into the room when Rosaleen had gone to the door and closed it. Niamh, however, had hold of the door jamb and the door closed on her fingers. Pat took her off to hospital as it seems that two fingers are broken.

OUTSIDE THE CLASSROOM 2002 Education Act	Not all teaching goes on inside the classroom. Nursery classes have been used to operating an outside classroom for many years (most nurseries in the 1970s and 1980s had outside areas set up for children to continue free play). Since the introduction of the Foundation Stage curriculum most reception classrooms, in recognition of how young children learn, now offer an outside classroom too. Of course, the potential for accidents is greater in an environment that enables freedom of movement for children. Add to this environment resources that move – such as bicycles, trucks, cars and buggies – and the risk factor for accidents increases. Higher risk factors are also apparent in other learning environments outside the classroom, such as the hall (PE, dance, drama or music) or playground and fields (games and PE).

INCIDENT 10: ADAM	Rugby is a strong sport at Eden Grammar School for Boys. The school has won many trophies and proudly displays them in the foyer together with pictures of the teams. They have been lucky and have not had many serious accidents – up to now the most serious has been a broken arm. Members of staff responsible for teaching the boys rugby have attended professional development courses regarding health and safety and the school has introduced safety equipment including helmets. In this incident, however, even the helmet didn't protect and Adam, a Year 9 boy, is carried off the field with a suspected broken neck and no feeling in his arms and legs. He's taken to hospital where his parents' and the school's worst fears are confirmed. Adam has a broken neck.

All schools have insurance to cover general accidents but, normally, for this to be valid, a paid member of staff should be the 'responsible person' and with the children at all times. For this reason, trainee teachers are not able to manage breaktime supervision by themselves, or PE (where children are climbing or using apparatus). However, the introduction of the outside classroom as part of the ongoing provision for young children means that, sometimes, trainee teachers are likely to be the only adult outside with a group of children. Head teachers are ultimately responsible and are expected to be aware of their insurance cover expectations.

INCIDENT 11: MICHAEL	'There I [Year 3 teacher] am, standing in position in PE. The children are on the climbing frame and I've told them – don't go over the top, it's dangerous. What does Michael do? Right over the top. He nearly hits his head on the ceiling! How can I stop that sort of child doing what he wants?'

SCHOOL JOURNEYS, EDUCATIONAL VISITS AND RISK ASSESSMENTS

Where the provision for children's learning is taking place away from the regular school environment, then teachers have less control over the situation. School journeys and educational visits are important in continuing children's development. In 2002 a tragedy occurred when 10-year-old Max Palmer died when he jumped into a pool at Glenridding Beck in Cumbria. He was accompanying his mother on a school trip, and although the teacher and his mother were present and tried to save him, they couldn't. This accident brought into sharp focus the importance of risk assessments. Good practice had already been identified in government publications, but not many followed the practice of writing risk assessments. Following the tragedy, websites[1] have been set up to continue reminding teachers of their responsibility. In particular, the Health and Safety Executive identifies ten questions

10 vital questions

If you are involved – in any way – with an educational visit, you'll want to know the most important questions to ask. The following ten questions cover the main arrangements that should be in place for a visit. These questions are important whether you're a parent, child, helper, leader, head teacher or governor. They are equally relevant to visits run by youth organisations.

1 What are the main objectives of the visit?
2 What is Plan B if the main objectives can't be achieved?
3 What could go wrong? Does the risk assessment cover:
   • The main activity
   • Plan B
   • Travel arrangements
   • Emergency procedures
   • Staff numbers, gender and skill mixes
   • Generic and site-specific hazards and risks (including for Plan B)

- Variable hazards (including environmental and participants' personal abilities and the 'cut off' points).

4 What information will be provided for parents?

5 What consents will be sought?

6 What opportunities will parents have to ask questions (including any arrangements for a parents' meeting)?

7 What assurances are there of the competencies of the leader or leaders?

8 What are the communication arrangements?

9 What are the arrangements for supervision, both during activities and during 'free time' – is there a Code of Conduct?

10 What are the arrangements for monitoring and reviewing the visit?

(http://www.hse.gov.uk accessed December 06)

CHILD PROTECTION

Children Act 1989; *Every Child Matters* (DfES 2004); Children Act 2004

Parents, in effect, give schools the authority to act *in loco parentis*. Teachers should take independent action to deal with emergencies, and they have a general duty to act independently in respect of suspected abuse at home. The law recognises that reasonable action may be defined as the action taken by a parent. It is most important that teachers are aware of national guidelines, follow school policies and are members of a professional body, who may protect them in the event of accusations of negligence or misconduct. Every school is required to have a Child Protection Policy and it is the individual teacher's professional responsibility to be aware of this and to follow it. This policy may refer to 'safeguarding' children rather than to child protection.

INCIDENT 12: CLARE	Clare, a Year 3 child, announces brightly that Granddad has arrived. 'He lets me sleep in his bed!'

The school has a responsibility to protect children from harm. Its policy should specify designated teachers and procedures for notifying social services departments, the NSPCC and police where there are concerns over a pupil's safety. Such concerns are bound to stem from the observations of the class teacher – marked behavioural changes, or bite marks, cigarette burns, and so on which may be visible when the child changes for PE. The school should have procedures for recording and reporting such incidents. The designated teacher should be properly trained and be aware of the role of local Area Child Protection Committees (ACPC). Schools' procedures must be in line with those adopted by the ACPC. Government also offers advice on working to promote children's welfare (DfES 2006c).

INCIDENT 13: MR W	Mrs W recently told you that she had left home with her children because she was being battered. She has moved into your school's catchment area. She told the head teacher and you that Mr W did not know where she was, and she wanted her address and that of the school kept from him. She

MR W *(continued)*	mentioned that there had been a court appearance and another one was pending. At lunchtime, Mr W arrives at your classroom accompanied by a large man with biceps bulging under the sleeves of his jacket. Mr W introduces him as his 'legal adviser'. Mr W says that he wishes to talk to his son. You refuse and he becomes aggressive, saying that the boy is in moral danger because of the mother's promiscuity. Mr W's arguments are punctuated by loud grunts of agreement from the legal adviser.

SCHOOL SECURITY
1998 Education (School Information) (England) Regulations; DfEE Circulars 7/99, 8/99

Schools must include information about school security in their annual reports. This requirement will now be covered within the School Profile, and many head teachers choose to publish information within their prospectuses, to reassure parents. Teachers need to be aware of all procedures regarding security, and carry out all requirements assiduously.

INCIDENT 14: JANIE	At the end of each school day, Grimwold Infant school children are let into the playground, where the children are told to stay until their parents meet them. Last Thursday you let your class out five minutes early. Janie ran out of the school, straight on to the main road, where she was knocked down by a lorry. Her mother arrived at the normal time. Later, Janie's mother demanded an explanation from you and threatened court action.

CONCLUSION

Health and safety are important parts of the duty of care that teachers have towards children. Although the final responsibility lies with the head teacher, it is still important that other employees in school are aware of their responsibility, for the head teacher cannot be everywhere. Accidents happen, and may result in investigation where negligence is found against individual employees and/or the head teacher. It is important to note that volunteers or trainee teachers or students cannot be left completely in charge. If accidents happen with no paid employee identified as responsible then insurance policies may not be valid.

Health and safety of children mean that the head teacher may be unable to provide support for individuals (see Chapter 3 Equal Opportunities). Support will always be sought from the Local Authority in these cases. Teachers' responsibilities are covered in more depth in Chapter 5 Employment.

FURTHER GUIDANCE

Further non-statutory guidance and amplification may be found in:
The Responsibilities of School Governors for Health and Safety, ISBN 0 717604365, published by HSE Books,1992.
Managing Health and Safety in Schools, ISBN 0 7176 0770 4, published by HSE Books, 1995.
Safety in Science Education, DfEE 1996. This supersedes previous safety guidance in science issued by the Department.

RESPONSE TO INCIDENT 9: NIAMH	Accidents happen! This sort of incident can be avoided, but not always, and as long as care has been taken in making sure that children are aware of the possibility of trapped fingers, and the teacher was managing the situation appropriately, then blame cannot be attributed. It is likely that following this incident the head teacher, with the senior management team and governing body, will carry out a further risk assessment which may suggest that some sort of safety mechanism be fitted to the doors. These young children would need supporting following this sort of trauma. Rosaleen needs to know she isn't to blame, other children who saw the incident need to understand the situation, and Niamh needs help to cope with her feelings, particularly toward Rosaleen.

RESPONSE TO INCIDENT 10: ADAM	This case is not a real one, but it is probably many secondary sports teachers' nightmare. Many secondary children have broken limbs in sporting accidents at school. For the teacher the important aspects are: • Is the activity within the children's capabilities? • Are the children playing team games well matched? • Have all reasonable procedures been applied to minimise the risk? Because the negligence in sporting injuries cases is often decided on the basis of the circumstances then being responsive to these three aspects is vital. Teachers should make sure that a risk assessment has been carried out and is frequently referred to and updated. Senior managers, the head teacher and the governing body would also need to be aware of the development of safety equipment. Once again, in a case such as Adam's, the statutory duty of care (Children's Act 1989) would consider if everything reasonable had been done in the circumstances for the safety and well-being of the child. How the incident occurred would be examined and the teacher's duties in teaching appropriate skills for rugby. If the teacher has taught them and a child chose not to follow rules he knows, the teacher has carried out his or her contractual duty. Numerous case law exists[2] but it is interesting that even when the claimant's position is upheld and the school is found to be negligent there is not necessarily a rush of cases brought to the courts. This is because teachers do act professionally and make certain that the children they work with are safe, even in potentially more dangerous activity.

RESPONSE TO INCIDENT 11: MICHAEL	When children are in danger on climbing frames, or in PE, it is important not to panic the rest of the children and put more of them into danger. Good practice suggests that you have agreed with the children what the stop signal is and have practised it. If you have followed this it is likely that Michael will follow the procedures and come down out of harm's way. What if he does hit his head on the ceiling and fall? Don't attempt to catch him as you may do both of yourselves harm. Avoid climbing up and trying to help down a child who has 'frozen'. Your actions might make them grab you and cause you both to fall. Talk calmly, bringing a child down to ground level (having got everyone else off).
	We would all like to shout at a child who does this, but even when the child is safe, consider how you might make sure the incident doesn't happen again, remembering that, legally, Michael is entitled to the PE curriculum. Although health and safety have priority, you cannot exclude a child from the curriculum indefinitely.
	A subtle comment has been made by the teacher here: 'that sort of child'. What is not clear from the description of this incident is to what the teacher is referring. As a statement it is not professional because whatever it is referring to, whether identifying a special need, or a cultural, socio-economic or racial aspect is inappropriate. It may be important to challenge the teacher's use of language.
	Knowing that Michael is black (Nigerian) and from a low socio-economic background, but that he does not have special needs may influence your decision on what to say in response to the colleague.

RESPONSE TO INCIDENT 12: CLARE	There is not enough information to make any decision about this. In this actual incident Clare's behaviour had been changing. She behaved differently when Granddad was around: not withdrawn, but quite the opposite. Over a period of time this behaviour pattern was noticed, and enough concern in the light of this statement meant that Child Protection agencies were called in.
	Importantly, if a child discloses anything to you, be aware that you can spoil the case by questioning. A simple rule of thumb is to repeat what the child (or young person) says rather than ask a question. This helps the child feel that s/he is being listened to, but does not make suggestions that could mean the Crown Prosecution Service cannot take up the case.

RESPONSE TO INCIDENT 13: MR W	Some situations cannot be handled alone. Get help immediately. Explain that Mr W and his adviser should speak to the head teacher and/or the deputy. Make sure that the police are alerted – most schools will have a policy for this type of situation. Be familiar with procedures before the event!

RESPONSE TO INCIDENT 14: JANIE	This is based on the case of Barnes v Hampshire County Council (1969). After an appeal to the House of Lords, Lord Pearson stated 'It was the duty of the School authorities not to release the children before closing time. Although a premature release would very seldom cause an accident, it foreseeably could, and in this case it did . . .'. Damages were awarded to the parents of the child. Basically, the school needs to have a fail-safe system for this sort of incident. What are the systems in your school for letting children out at the end of the day?

NOTES

1 http://www.schooltravelforum.com; http://www.hse.gov.uk
2 See in particular Affutu Nartay v Clarke (*The Times*, 9 February 1984) or Mountford v Newlands School (CA) [2007] EWCA Civ 21

5 Employment

Employment Rights Act
1996; Employment
Relations Act 1999

This section is principally concerned with the responsibilities of teachers and the legal framework which sustains them. But teachers have rights as well as duties. It is not suggested that any teacher should become a 'barrack-room lawyer', but a brief overview of some of the main areas which might become of concern to teachers is appropriate. Much of UK employment law is designed to comply with EU legal requirements and applies to teachers as it does to everyone else. For example, a scheme for maternity and parental leave found in the Employment Relations Act 1999 has been updated in the Employment Act 2002, and again in the Work and Families Act 2006, under Statutory Instrument 2006, No. 2014. Needless to say, this is not a full account of any aspect of the law on which you should rely if you encounter a difficulty. Employment law is a complex and specialised area. A union should be able to provide advice in most situations.

Teachers' employment conditions are set out in an annually updated document, *School Teachers' Pay and Conditions*, which clarifies the range of duties teachers may be asked to undertake. It is important to understand that these must be consistent with the contract. It is beyond the scope of this book to interpret this document and its implications for contracts, however, and I recommend that you ask for legal advice from one of the professional bodies if you need help. Teachers can often make erroneous complaints because they've interpreted the legal position wrongly. An example of this is the position of oral contracts. If a teacher is offered and accepts a job this can constitute a binding agreement on both parties. It does not have to be in writing. However, it is important to remember that there may be other aspects that affect the interpretation of the law, so before making formal complaints contact your professional body.

Since 2003 there have been workforce reforms going on in schools. In particular the introduction of PPA (Planning, Preparation and Assessment) time meant that all teachers in the maintained sector could expect 10 per cent of their teaching day to be in school, often with colleagues, but not working directly with children. At this time governing bodies are still trying to manage the budget to provide for this, and in some schools you may see teaching assistants 'delivering' teachers' plans, or subject specialists who are not trained teachers working with children, particularly in music and sport. This major change has been driven by the Training and Development Agency (TDA) whose previous leader, Ralph Tabberer, promoted the vision of professionals working together to educate children. This changes the idea of the 'heroic teacher' (Tabberer, NaPTEC Conference 2005) of the *Dead Poets Society*, and strengthens the idea of teams. However, there is an issue about expectations. Not all teaching assistants have had training, although they may be very experienced in working with children and bring a lot of knowledge to the task. As roles are agreed upon, and pay levels rise, it may mean that TAs will be expected to do more of the teachers' tasks. Many appear to be being paid at 'unqualified teacher' level (as defined in *School Teachers' Pay and Conditions Document 2007)* to cover games or Planning, Preparation and Assessment (PPA) time. As the workforce reform continues you will need to be clear about your role and the expectations of others, particularly if you are planning lessons for someone else who is not a qualified teacher to 'deliver'.

EMPLOYMENT PROTECTION

Teachers, like most other employees, are entitled either to a written contract or to a statement in writing of the main terms of their employment. Teachers with one year's continuous service generally have the right not to be unfairly dismissed. This includes 'constructive dismissal', when an employee leaves, but is justified in doing so because of the employer's conduct. If an employee is dismissed, it is for the employer to show the reason, and to show that it is one that the law recognises and that they have acted fairly in relying on it to dismiss the employee.

A teacher who has two years continuous service and is dismissed by reason of redundancy is entitled to compensation. Redundancy may arise if a school is closed, or if for demographic or other reasons there is a need for fewer staff. Unfair selection for redundancy may amount to unfair dismissal.

All teachers are strongly advised to affiliate to a professional association – at all levels of their teaching career. This career begins at the training level with the Training and Development Agency for Schools (TDA) using the term 'trainee teacher'. The major teaching unions will include legal fees and support within their members' entitlement. The variety of approaches to supporting members is extensive, with some including basic rules such as 'no striking' (e.g. PAT– the Professional Association of Teachers) and membership to different levels of teachers (e.g. NAHT – the National Association of Head Teachers).

INCIDENT 15: MELEK

Seven-year-old Melek Wallis arrives at school one morning with a bruise on her cheek. You sensitively enquire how it came to be there, and she tells you her mum did it. As she tells you this, Mrs Wallis appears at the door and, having overheard, denies it hotly. She demands your promise that you won't pass on 'such a terrible story'.

DISCIPLINARY RULES: GRIEVANCES

School Standards and Framework Act 1998; Employment Relations Act 1999

The governors of a school have responsibilities for staff matters, whether or not they are also the employers. All schools must have disciplinary rules and procedures for staff and arrangements for hearing staff grievances. The governors may suspend a member of staff on full pay and can require the LA to dismiss him or her. The procedures will usually include an appeal process. The procedures and their operation must be fair and reasonable. Teachers generally have the right to be accompanied by a union representative or fellow teacher at any disciplinary hearing. Once again, membership of a professional organisation will ensure that the individual teacher has access to advice and resources, if he or she has a grievance.

INCIDENT 16: STEFAN	Stefan (Year 1) has just joined the school, having been permanently excluded from another school. He does not have a statement of special educational need but is on the register at School Action, as his behaviour is aggressive, particularly towards adults. Stefan is working with you in the ICT suite with his new class and two other adults (one an ICT technician). He gets frustrated with his partner because he wants to type, and when you go over to remonstrate with him he argues with you, loses his temper and starts hitting you.

DISCRETIONARY ELEMENTS OF TEACHERS' PAY

School Teachers' Pay and Conditions 1998; School Teachers' Pay and Conditions 2007

Governors can decide discretionary elements of teachers' pay, and the grade to which new non-teaching staff will be appointed. The profession is about to enter the era of 'fast-track' pay. This will be decided upon by the head, and validated by external threshold assessors. Membership of a professional body will give access to advice and resources for the individual teacher.

QUALIFIED TEACHER STATUS

Education Reform Act 1988; Teaching and Higher Education Act 1998; 2000 and 2002 Education Acts; School Teachers' Pay and Conditions Document 2007

Employment as a teacher in state schools is normally restricted to individuals with qualified teacher status (QTS). The main exceptions are licensed teachers and overseas-trained teachers, who are in effect undergoing on-the-job training, leading to QTS. Teachers in state schools, and in most independent schools, must successfully complete an induction period of not less than three terms and pass the recently introduced National Skills Test. However, the 2002 Education Act enables schools to make use of a wider range of expertise from beyond the school's normal boundaries, so that schools can share staff with one another and can make use of expertise from other sectors, such as further education. This is expected to help schools develop partnerships with one another and support the sharing of expertise. The Act also makes clear that schools have to make greater use of support staff in the classroom, and clarifies the roles of those with QTS and those without.

The TDA, with the GTC, has developed the idea of Continuing Professional Development (CPD). The QTS standards are the only standards available so far. At the time of writing the TDA have developed standards for teachers throughout their careers and these will be informing the performance management aspects of teachers' careers (the standards are described in Chapter 4).[1] In London the Chartered London Teacher standards are being used to enable CPD.[2] Schools had to set a 'staffing structure' in December 2005 which outlined new Teaching and Learning Resource positions and scales of payment.

INCIDENT 17: FIGHT, FIGHT, FIGHT!	You are on playground duty with another teacher. She has gone over to speak to some children at the other end of the playground, when – near to you – a fight breaks out. Two boys from year 8 are surrounded by a large number of children chanting 'Fight, fight, fight!' What do you do as the nearest/only adult available?

APPRAISAL

1986 Education Act; Statutory Instrument 1/1511 Education School Teacher Appraisal Regulations 1991; 2005 Education Act; Education (School Teachers Performance Management) (England) Regulations 2006

All qualified teachers employed full-time, or on 40 per cent full-time contracts of not less than one year, are subject to appraisal of their performance, on a two-year cycle. Schools now have Performance Management cycles for all their staff (including non-teaching staff) and, with the development of the staffing structure mentioned above, teachers other than the head teacher may be responsible for managing this. It is the responsibility of the governing body to see that the policy for performance management is clearly set out within the expectations of the law. They are also responsible for managing the performance management of the head teacher.

Performance management will be used as evidence in cases of competence. If a complaint is brought by a parent or member of staff to the head teacher, or if the head teacher is concerned about the ability of a teacher to carry out the duties expected of them, then a panel of governors may be asked to hear evidence to support the dismissal of a member of staff. The teacher has the right to appeal.

DISCRIMINATION

Equal Pay Act 1970; Sex Discrimination Act 1975; Race Relations Act 1976; Disability Discrimination Act 1995

The Equal Pay Act 1970, Sex Discrimination Act 1975, the Race Relations Act 1976 and the Disability Discrimination Act 1995 (DDA) provide strong protection in these areas, starting with the recruitment process and continuing throughout the employment relationship up to and including any dismissal process. An unfair dismissal may therefore attract legal action both under ordinary employment protection and anti-discrimination law. The DDA carries with it a detailed Code of Practice and imposes an obligation on employers to make reasonable adjustments for persons with disability. Teachers must familiarise themselves with the basic principles of anti-discrimination law which they must operate when dealing with pupils and which, in turn, protect them in their dealings with their employers.

THE WORKING RELATIONSHIP

Employers are under a general legal duty, apart from statutory obligations under the Health and Safety at Work Act 1974 and other legislation, to take reasonable steps to provide a safe system of work and a safe workplace. Like any other person on school premises, teachers are entitled to this standard of protection against reasonably foreseeable physical injury. Recently, claims by teachers for damages for work-related stress have not been uncommon. The Court of Appeal has reiterated that employers are only liable to take steps to protect teachers against reasonably foreseeable harm. Although indications of impending harm to an employee's mental health have to be sufficiently plain for any reasonable employer to realise that he should do something about it, an employer has to be pro-active (and not merely re-active) in looking out for signs of stress in their employees, and should keep themselves up to date with developing knowledge of occupational stress and protective measures to alleviate it.[3]

Trust and confidence

Underlying any employment relationship is a duty, implied by law, of trust and confidence, mutual to employer and employee. This is very often invoked by employees in a wide variety of circumstances. Arbitrariness or capriciousness or lack of even-handedness by the employer may be a breach of this contractual obligation.

Privacy

Article 8 of the European Convention for the Protection of Human Rights and Fundamental Freedoms, imported into domestic law by the Human Rights Act 1998,[4] provides that 'Everyone has the right to respect for his private and family life, his home and his correspondence'. Interference with this right may only be justified if legally based and proportionate for the protection of 'national security, public safety or the economic well-being of the country, for the prevention of disorder or crime, for the protection of health or morals, or for the protection of the rights and freedoms of others'. There are obvious implications in the areas of surveillance in the workplace and interception of electronic communications. This is a complex and developing area of law, and it is not proposed here to do anything other than draw attention to its existence.

LEARNING RESOURCES: COPYRIGHT

Copyright, Designs and Patents Act 1988

Teachers must be aware of the school's arrangements for copying material. Licences are required for reprographics and recording of broadcasts in certain circumstances. The legislation covers copying of printed and magnetic materials and licences for use of computer software and broadcasts. Schools (and therefore teachers) are required to keep full records of certain types of copying.

Photocopiers have become a standard and necessary tool in the resource base of schools. It is very easy to photocopy materials for children to use, and very often materials provided by publishers or on the internet clearly state that they may be copied for educational use. However, many do not come with that option and teachers should be careful about what they choose to copy. 'Copying' means in any way – including being written out by hand, photocopied, recorded by tape or CD, and photographed. Photocopying pages from a story book for thirty children in the class will be contravening the copyright laws if the school or LA does not have permission or special arrangements.

SAFETY

Health and Safety at Work Act 1974; Control of Substances Hazardous to Health Regulations 1994; Ionising Radiations Regulations 1985; Statutory Instrument 1989/635

Teachers must use all resources safely. In secondary schools this would include materials used in science e.g. low-level radioactive materials, and technology e.g. electric saws. Teachers can expect secondary school children to have some skill in using resourses they would have met in the primary school, which would include use of scissors, knives and other design and technology tools, such as glue guns. In the secondary school, where teachers are trained to focus on one or two subjects, health and safety is part of their ongoing training, but it can easily be forgotten for primary teachers, or those secondary teachers supervising other subjects. There is an expectation that risk assessments will have been carried out for general work, or specific activities such as school journeys and visits (see Chapter 4) or design and technology.

CONCLUSION

There are two aspects of their employment for which a teacher can be held responsible: their discipline and their competence. If there is a complaint, the head teacher should investigate under either area (or sometimes both) and will report to a panel of the governing body, convened for this purpose, to hear the grievance or complaint. The head teacher should not involve governors (except perhaps the Chair of Governors) so as not to 'taint' them. It is important that the governing body knows a complaint or grievance has arisen, but not the details or the names of the parties. With a child protection issue, an investigation may be delayed if the investigation itself might warn the alleged perpetrator. Sometimes a teacher or member of staff will even be allowed to stay in post until the appropriate authorities (e.g. police and child protection authorities) have been notified.

The teaching profession is a dynamic profession. There are changes happening in it all the time, many of which are developing the robustness of the profession. With the development of the General Teaching Council for England and establishment of strong professional bodies, including unions, and the continuous research practised by Higher Education bodies (especially Teacher Education establishments) this rigour will continue. Recent changes have meant that more teachers leave the profession and change career but, similarly, others join the teaching profession, having established careers elsewhere. Perhaps it is no longer a 'job for life' but the role of the teacher as an important and valuable educator will never be lost. Employment of teachers, their rights and expectations will always be changing, but in our global community we should be able to find out more easily how society expects us to behave.

RESPONSE TO INCIDENT 15: MELEK	Whatever Mrs Wallis says, the duty of the teacher is to protect the child. If any suspicions were aroused, it would be his/her duty to report it to the head teacher. In fact, anything a teacher says (even it turns out to be wrong) to concerned parties, e.g. the head teacher, Education Welfare Officer, is protected. LA procedures should be scrupulously followed. Who is the nominated child protection person at the school?
	If a child discloses anything to a teacher, that teacher has a duty to manage the situation and not transfer the responsibility. Never promise to keep a secret if asked to – a child may have lost trust in adults because of abuse, and to promise something you cannot keep will add to that loss of trust. Importantly, avoid questioning a child, as those questions can suggest a response from a child and spoil the disclosure. If a child discloses anything to you, rather than questioning, try repeating what the child has said. In this way you are appearing supportive but not 'tainting the evidence'.

RESPONSE TO INCIDENT 16: STEFAN	Stefan is a child with a special educational need, which the adults working with him will be aware of. His permanent exclusion from his previous school will also have alerted the staff to his possible behaviour, although a child cannot be permanently excluded because he has a special educational need. In this incident the head teacher had a duty to investigate the incident by questioning all involved, including the child (possibly with his parents). If a child hits a teacher, the incident should be recorded and the consequences considered.
	If a child does hit you, the important aspect is to appear non-aggressive and if possible to step back from the child. In some areas, such as a classroom or an ICT suite, it may not be possible to step back. People naturally raise hands or arms in defence, but to onlookers this can be interpreted differently. If a teacher is angry this will add to the interpretation of others – children often remember the teacher being cross with an individual. It is important to remain calm – the child has lost his temper, not you.
	Incidents where a child or teacher is accused of hitting will need to be dealt with sensitively. Head teachers will usually take advice from the LA, and teachers are advised to contact their professional associations.

RESPONSE TO INCIDENT 17: FIGHT, FIGHT, FIGHT!	Your first action must be to send some children for help – to the staff room, or the head teacher. Before wading in to stop the fight, consider your safety and the safety of the other children. Try using your authority as a teacher first (develop a good 'stop' voice). When other adults come you may be able to stop the two by pulling them apart, but trying to put yourself between two children fighting is likely to cause you injury. Moving the audience may help, but often fighters are no longer hearing the onlookers.
	Consider prevention as the better course. Within the standards for QTS are those which consider strategies for behaviour and the learning environment. Most schools recognise the playground as a learning environment and will have organised games set up. Teachers on playground duty can encourage children to play simple games together – such as singing and dancing games. Many schools have 'buddy' schemes where children, often identified by a piece of clothing (cap or band), will play with those who may be lonely, bullied or bullies. Check your school policies – or suggest ideas if they are not in place in your school.

Don't forget: look after yourself too. Join a professional body, keep up to date on legal matters by taking a professional journal, read the *Times Educational Supplement*, and develop your professional persona.

NOTES

1 http://www.tda.gov.uk/upload/resources/pdf/d/draft_revised_standards_framework_jan_2007.pdf

2   Further information is available at www.clt.ac.uk

3   Hatton v Sutherland CA 2002 and Barber v Somerset County Council (2004) UKHL 13.

4   Article 8: Right to respect for private and family life. Online: http://conventions.coe.int/Treaty/en/Treaties/Html/005.htm

Conclusion

The material contained in this book is intended to show that, whatever period of your teaching career you are in, you are part of an organisation where your responsibilities and your rights are complex and reflect each other. Your school is subject to the law and much that you do as a teacher is, therefore, governed by law. There are generally very good reasons for following school policies carefully, and these reasons are connected with legally enforceable requirements. For this reason it is important that you know what your schools' policies are and, more importantly, how they may inform your practice.

ACTION	When was the last time you read your school's policies?
	Have you been given copies of all the policies?
	What did you do with them?
	Turn to your policy documents (teachers are often given a folder with copies of the policies in it). For each policy, when you have read it, identify *briefly* on an A4 sheet what the policy means for you in your teaching position. If you are a class teacher, what does it mean for you teaching your class? (If yours is a Year 1 class, the policy is likely to apply differently from the way it would apply to a Year 6 class.) If you are a senior manager, with a whole-school responsibility, consider how you should be managing or promoting the policy. If you are not, who should be? If you are a secondary teacher working within subject areas do you have all the policies that relate to your subject areas? What about your responsibility when you 'cover' for a colleague, or begin to teach in a different subject area?
	Some policies may be over five years old. Consider talking to your head teacher or other senior manager about whether there is a newer version, or about the policy being updated. But be warned: you might be asked to do it!

Teachers' greatest worries centre on the safety and welfare of the children in their care. Accidents are rare, but they do occur. Although there may be a perception that we are moving towards a 'blame' culture, it is important to recognise that support is available. In most cases, if you have made a mistake, talking to your line manager is a priority. We all try to cover and excuse ourselves, but keeping to the facts of the situation, without suggesting fault (including taking the blame yourself) is vital. Similarly, talking to your professional association is very important – and they will help. If you are not already a member, you need to consider joining one of the professional organisations to ensure your own protection. The internet has become a hugely supportive resource, although the data it provides often needs to be interpreted – or there may be too much of it! In our busy teaching lives it may not be as supportive as it appears.

Finally, return to the 'Reflection' box at the end of the Introduction. Are your answers still the same? Do you have any areas that you need to improve on to enhance your knowledge of this wonderful profession?

Bibliography and further reading

Bubb, S. (2004) *The Insider's Guide to Early Professional Development: Succeed in your first five years as a teacher (TES Career Guides)*. London: RoutledgeFalmer.

Bubb, S. (2005) *Helping Teachers Develop*. London: Paul Chapman Publishing.

Bubb, S. (2007) *Successful Induction for New Teachers: A guide for NQTs and induction tutors, coordinators and mentors*. London: Sage/Paul Chapman.

Cheminais, R. (2006) *Every Child Matters: A practical guide for teachers*. London: David Fulton Publishers.

DCSF (2007) *14–19 Education and skills: Qualifications*. Online: http://www.dfes.gov.uk/14-19/index.cfm?sid=3 (accessed 17 August 2007).

DFE (1994) *Code of Practice on the Identification and Assessment of Special Educational Needs*. London: DFE.

DfEE/QCA (1999) *The National Curriculum: Handbook for primary school teachers*. London: DfEE/QCA.

DfES (2001) *Special Educational Needs Code of Practice*. London: DfES.

DfES (2002) *Qualifying to Teach: Professional standards for Qualified Teacher Status and requirements for Initial Teacher Training*. London: TTA.

DfES (2003) *Excellence and Enjoyment: A strategy for primary schools*. London: DfES.

DfES (2004a) *Every Child Matters: Change for children*. London: DfES.

DfES (2004b) *14–19 Curriculum and Qualifications Reform*. London: DfES.

DfES (2005) *Secondary National Strategy for School Improvement 2005–6*. London: DfES.

DfES (2006a) *The Primary Framework for Literacy and Mathematics*. London: DfES.

DfES (2006b) *5-Year Strategic Plan and 2006/07 Annual Plan: Summary for Schools*. London: DfES.

DfES (2006c) *Working Together to Safeguard Children: A guide to inter-agency working to safeguard and promote the welfare of children*. London: DfES.

DfES (2006d) *A Short Guide to the Education and Inspections Act 2006.*. Online: http://www.dfes.gov.uk/publications/educationandinspectionsact/ (accessed 17 August 2007).

DfES (2006e) *A condensed Key Stage 3: Designing a flexible curriculum 2006 update*. London: DfES.

Document Summary Service (2005) *Teachers' Legal Liabilities and Responsibilities: The Bristol Guide*. Bristol: University of Bristol, Graduate School of Education.

Frederickson, N. and Cline, T. (2002) *Special Educational Needs, Inclusion and Diversity: A Textbook*. Buckingham: Open University Press.

Great Britain, Education Service Advisory Committee (1992) *The Responsibilities of School Governors for Health and Safety*. London: HMSO.

Great Britain, Education Service Advisory Committee (1995) *Managing Health and Safety in Schools*. London: HSE Books.

Great Britain, Education Service Advisory Committee (1996) *Safety in Science Education*. London: HMSO.

GTC (2005) *What We Do: The General Teaching Council for England (introductory leaflet)*. Birmingham: GTC.

Harris, N.S. with Pearce, P. and Johnston, S. (1991) *The Legal Context of Teaching*. London: Longman.

Ofsted (1996) *The Implementation of the Code of Practice for Pupils with Special Educational Needs*. London: HMSO.

Ofsted (1997) *The SEN Code of Practice: Two Years On*. London: HMSO.

Ofsted (2005) *Annual Report of Her Majesty's Chief Inspector of Schools 2004/05*. Ofsted: London.

Pollard, A. (ed.) (1996) *Readings for Reflective Teaching in the Primary School*. London: Cassell Education.

1.6 Council for the Accreditation of Teacher Education, 'Criteria for initial teacher training in England: primary phase'. From: Department for Education (1993) *The Initial Training of Primary School Teachers: New Criteria for Course Approval*. London: DFE.

1.8 James Calderhead, 'Competence and the complexities of teaching'. From: Calderhead, J. (1994) 'Can the complexities of teaching be accounted for in terms of competences? Contrasting views of professional practice from research and policy' (mimeo, ESRC Research Conference seminar on teacher competence 1–2). (*See also* Calderhead, J. (1988) *Teachers' Professional Learning*. London: Falmer.)

2.4 Richard Bowe and Stephen Ball with Ann Gold, 'Three contexts of policy making'. From: Bowe, R. and Ball, S. with Gold, A. (1992) *Reforming Education and Changing Schools*. London: Routledge.

2.5 Len Barton, Elizabeth Barrett, Geoff Whitty, Sheila Miles and John Furlong, 'Teacher education and professionalism'. From: Barton, L., Barrett, E., Whitty, G., Miles, S. and Furlong J. (1994) 'Teacher education and teacher professionalism in England: some emerging issues'. *British Journal of Sociology Education* 15(4): 529–31.

3.6 David Hopkins and Robert Bollington, 'Teacher appraisal'. From: Hopkins, D. and Bollington, R. (1989) 'Teacher appraisal for professional development: a review of research'. *Cambridge Journal of Education* 19(2): 165–79.

4.4 Michael Apple, 'Deskilling and intensification'. From: Apple, M.W. (1993) *Official Knowledge: Democratic Education in a Conservative Age*. London: Routledge.

Pollard, A. (ed.) (2002) *Readings for Reflective Teaching*. London: Continuum.

2.4 James Calderhead, 'Competence and the complexities of teaching'. From: Calderhead, J. (1994) 'Can the complexities of teaching be accounted for in terms of competences? Contrasting views of professional practice from research and policy' (mimeo, ESRC Research Conference seminar on teacher competence 1–2). (*See also* Calderhead, J. (1988) *Teachers' Professional Learning*. London: Falmer).

18.4 Richard Bowe and Stephen Ball with Ann Gold, 'Three contexts of policy making'. From: Bowe, R. and Ball, S. with Gold, A. (1992) *Reforming Education and Changing Schools*. London: Routledge.

QCA (2002) *Designing and Timetabling the Primary Curriculum*. London: QCA.

QCA (2005) *Religious Education and Collective Worship: An analysis of 2004 SACRE Reports*. London: QCA.

School Teachers' Pay and Conditions Document 2007. Online: http://www.teachernet.gov.uk/_doc/11807/web_stpc_2007.pdf (accessed 6 September 2007).

Spooner, W. (2006) *The SEN Handbook for Trainee Teachers, NQTs and Teaching Assistants*. London: David Fulton.

Tabberer, R. (2005) Address made to NaPTEC Conference delegates, September 2005, Oxford.

TDA (2007a) *Professional Standards for Teachers: Qualified Teacher Status*. London: TDA.

TDA (2007b) *Professional Standards for Teachers in England from September 2007*. Online: http://www.tda.gov.uk/upload/resources/pdf/s/standards_framework.pdf (accessed 17 August 2007).

TDA (2007c) *Professional Standards for Teachers: Post-threshold*. London: TDA.

CIRCULARS REFERRED TO IN THE TEXT

A full list of all current and superseded circulars is available from the DfES website: www.dfes.gov.uk and from http://www.teachernet.gov.uk/Events calendar/

DES Circulars

8/86	Education (No. 2) Act 1986
7/87	Education (No. 2) Act 1986: Further Guidance
11/88	Admission of Pupils to County and Voluntary Schools
1/89	Local arrangements for the consideration of school complaints
2/89	Education Reform Act 1988: Charges for School Activities
5/89	The Education Reform Act 1988: The School Curriculum and Assessment

DFE Circular	14/89	The Education (School Curriculum and Related Information) Regulations 1989
	15/89	Education Reform Act 1988: Temporary Exceptions from the National Curriculum
	18/89	The Education (Teachers) Regulations 1989
	7/90	Management of the School Day
	11/90	Staffing for Pupils with Special Educational Needs
	6/91	Implementation of More Open Enrolment in Primary Schools
	12/91	School Teacher Appraisal

Provisions of the Education (Schools) Act 1992 in England Revised Annex to Circular. Summary of Responsibilities in Respect of School (Replaces 7/93: annexes appearing in Inspection Circular 7/93.)

	9/93	Protection of Children: Disclosure of Criminal Background of Those with Access to Children (Joint Circular with Home Office)
	15/93	The Use of School Premises and the Incorporation of Governing Bodies of LEA Maintained Schools
	1/94	Religious Education and Collective Worship
	2/94	Local Management of Schools
	3/94	The Development of Special Schools
	5/94	Education Act 1993: Sex Education in Schools
	6/94	The Organisation of Special Educational Provision
	8/94	Pupils with Problems: Pupil Behaviour and Discipline
	4/95	Drug Prevention and Schools
DfEE Circulars	11/95	Misconduct of Teachers and Workers with Children and Young Persons (Replaces Administrative Memoranda 2/90)
	7/96	Use of Supply Teachers
	10/96	Education (School Premises) Regulations 1996
	1/97	Reports on Pupils' Achievements in Primary Schools in 1996/97
	3/97	What the Disability Discrimination Act Means For Schools and LEAs (DDA) 1995
	7/97	Specialist Schools – Education Partnership for 21st Century
	6/98	Baseline Assessment for Pupils Starting Primary School
	7/98	School Prospectuses in Primary Schools 1998/9 onwards
	8/98	School Prospectuses in Secondary Schools 1998/9 onwards
	10/98	Section 550A of the Education Act 1996: The Use of Force to Control or Restrain Pupils
	11/98	Target-setting in Schools
	12/98	School Admissions: Interim Guidance
	15/98	New Framework Governing Bodies
	2/99	Qualifications under Section 400 of the Education Act 1996
	5/99	Induction Period for New Teachers
	6/99	Schools Causing Concern
	7/99	Governors' Annual Reports in Primary Schools

8/99   Governors' Annual Reports in Secondary Schools
9/99   Organisation of School Places
10/99   Social Inclusion: Pupil Support
11/99   Social Inclusion: the LEA Role in Pupil Support
12/99   School Teachers' Pay and Conditions of Employment 1999

DfES Circular   15/2000   The Education (School Records) Regulations 2000
                       92/2004   Drugs: Guidance for Schools

WEBSITES
http://www.askatl.org.uk/	Association of Teachers and Lecturers
http://www.clt.ac.uk	Chartered London Teachers
http://cowo.culham.ac.uk/guidance/	*Collective worship resources*
http://www.cre.gov.uk	Commission for Racial Equality
http://www.dfes.gov.uk	Department for Education and Skills
http://www.dfes.gov.uk/publications/ guidanceonthelaw	*DfES guidance on the law*
http://www.emplaw.co.uk	*British employment law*
http://www.governet.gov.uk	*DfES support for governors*
http://www.gtce.org.uk	General Teaching Council, England
http://www.hse.gov.uk	Health and Safety Executive
http://www.naht.org.uk/	National Association of Head Teachers
http://www.nasuwt.org.uk/	National Association of Schoolmasters Union of Women Teachers (NASUWT)
http://www.pat.org.uk/	Professional Association of Teachers (PAT) affiliated with Professional Association of Nursery Nurses (PANN) and Professionals Allied to Teaching (PAtT)
http://www.qca.org.uk	Qualifications and Curriculum Authority
http://www.qca.org.uk/7659.html	QCA Assessment for Learning
http://www.reonline.org.uk/	*Religious education resources*
http://www.standards.dfes.gov.uk/	*Government site devoted to raising standards in schools*
http://www.schooltravelforum.com	*Advice on school journeys and visits*
http://www.tda.gov.uk	Training and Developmental Agency for schools
http://www.tda.gov.uk/teachers/ professionalstandards.aspx	TDA Professional Standards 2007 onwards
http://www.teachernet.gov.uk	*DfES support for teachers*
http://www.teachernet.gov.uk/ Eventscalendar/	*DfES Key educational events in next 12 months*
http://www.teachernet.gov.uk/ management/payand performance/pay/	*Teachers' pay information*
http://www.teachers.org.uk/	National Union of Teachers (NUT)

Index